SOMETHING LOST BEHIND THE RANGES
Memoirs of a Traveler in Peru

Phyllis Mazzocchi

TRAVEL GRAVEL
LOS ANGELES

Travel Gravel, 6922 Paseo Del Serra, Los Angeles, CA 90068

www.travelgravel.com

ISBN: 0985521805
ISBN-13: 978-0-9855218-0-6

Something hidden. Go and find it.

Go and look behind the ranges.

Something lost behind the ranges.

Lost and waiting for you. Go!

—Rudyard Kipling, *The Explorer*

SOMETHING LOST BEHIND THE RANGES

CONTENTS

PREFACE

The romance of Machu Picchu has held many in its sway—be it for the sheer beauty, the logical impossibility of its locale, or the visceral sense of the sacred that is evoked as we are stilled by the sight of it.

Perhaps it is the mystery of that which is never fully revealed that intoxicates us with its charm, continuing to hold us captivated by virtue of its obfuscation. Perhaps such stalwart vestiges are evidence that our intentions made visible prevail, leaving their mark behind to be inherited by others as recovered and revisioned through new eyes.

Like the bygone cities that have survived the test of time, we are, in our quest of them, reminded of that which remains subsistent within ourselves.

1
ARRIVAL, WARNINGS, AND DREAMS

Remnants of stone,
like dreams,
rise to the surface
to speak
and make known

"Turismo," I respond to the immigration officer, who eyeballs me from beneath his tilted cap with grave curiosity as he inquires of my purpose for visiting Peru. The fact that I am not with an organized tour group, nor staying with a friend, seems to arouse his suspicion. Flipping his thumb through the pages of my passport like a Blackjack dealer preparing to split a deck of cards, he examines my documents and then hesitates, as if weighing his decision thoughtfully. For a brief moment, I almost believe he may not let me into the country.

A "state of siege" has been declared in Peru due to the recent bombings by the revolutionary terrorist group Sendero Luminoso (otherwise known as *The Shining Path*) and I am traveling here by myself despite a Travel Advisory warning issued by the U.S. State Department. Notwithstanding these inauspicious conditions, it is just my timing to be in Peru. From the moment I spotted that first fateful photograph of Machu Picchu, the archaeological site reputed to have been the legendary "Lost City of the Incas," in an old issue of National Geographic Magazine, I was compelled to go there. The powerful imagery that enticed me off the printed page that day appeared in the guise of two sugarloaf pinnacles, a larger and a smaller; their soft-shouldered edges roofed in a mossy green growth reminiscent of the jungle-worn summits of Hawaii or the Far East. Side by side, they stood in what I saw as a protective posture, maintaining their vigilance in elegant stillness over a gray stone city that fell in stepped terraces above the sheer cliff. So thoughtful were the curved walls mated to the hillside, so kind was the sculpting of one precise stone upon the other that in the face of the hunter's mark prevailed.

Safely hidden from harm's way in the arms of its mountain perch, Machu Picchu had successfully escaped the pillage of the Spanish conquest of 1532, maintaining its anonymity but for the locals until the American explorer Hiram Bingham discovered it in July of 1911. Bingham had followed a calling of his own, harkening to the stories of a golden city named Vilcabamba, purported to have been the preeminent capital of the Inca Empire. Fueled by a dogged determination and the romantic verve that characterizes those who are indefatigable in the pursuit of their vision, Bingham, an ex-Senator and Yale professor, set out with the tenacity of a Christopher Columbus making sail for the Americas, or an Arthurian knight in search of the Holy Grail.[1] In his pocket, he carried a crumpled piece of paper, scrawled with an excerpt from the author Rudyard Kipling's epic poem, *The Explorer*. The romanticism of the verse reveals the magnitude of the rapturous motivation that drove him:

> Something hidden. Go and find it.
> Go and look behind the ranges.
> Something lost behind the ranges.
> Lost and waiting for you. Go!
> —*Rudyard Kipling, The Explorer*

A fluttering of papers—and then at last, the sharp thud of a visa stamp assures me that all is well. "Welcome to Peru!" barks the immigration officer; while with a dismissive flip of the hand he waves me onwards to the terminal where I plan to spend the night. Such is the case that my early morning flight to Cusco, the Inca citadel 11,200 feet in the Andes that is the gateway to Machu Picchu, departs at 7:30am and I have planned to spend the wee hours of the morning at Lima airport, in lieu of a hotel. Following the recommendation as set forth in bold upper case letters in my guidebook, prudence suggests that I best be on line at the check-in counter at 5am, as a ticket and a reservation are no guarantee of getting on an airplane in Peru.

At one o'clock in the morning, it is a sanitary stillness that permeates the atmosphere at Jorge Chavez International Airport, belying the cause of the curfew certificate I have just been issued. Unobtrusively slipped between the pages of my passport, the document certified by the office of the "Commando Conjuncto de las Fuerzas Armadas" designates a 10pm curfew for tourists that I promptly breach upon my late arrival.

Seemingly devoid of all sound and motion until the deplaning of our flight, the Arrivals Terminal is temporarily resuscitated by the invasive clatter of emergent passengers whose feisty burst of energy breathes a bit of life into the barren airport, but just barely. Bypassing luggage claim by reason of my carry-on, I sprint through the exit door and am promptly met with a large over-sized poster conspicuous to my direct line of sight. Distinguished against the yellow-ochre walls seasoned with wear, it is the one spot of vigor that steals my eye. "Comet Halley in Peru!" proclaims the broad headline, punctuated in a three-dimensional blockbuster font against the backdrop of a blackened sky speckled with stars. A comet of herculean proportions streaks diagonally into the foreground; its luminescent tail of cobalt blue trailing behind it in a blaze of motion. As the laws of synchronicity would have it, I have arranged my trip at a time when the fabled Halley's Comet will make its cyclical re-appearance for the first time in seventy-two years, exacting its closest point to earth for a period of three days, right here in the southern hemisphere of the Americas. I have a knack for the timing of such recurrent three-day celestial events, having once arrived in Hardwar, India during the three high holy days of the *Kumbha Mela*, a festival that honors the transiting of the planet Jupiter through the constellation of Aquarius, once every twelve years. Entirely coincident to my loosely planned schedule, I was to happen upon town at the very peak of the celebration when over a million pilgrims descended upon the city of Hardwar to bathe in the Ganges and participate in ceremonial rite—resulting in a chaotic, but most memorable travel experience.

Finding the restroom, I change out of my jacket and sweater into a lighter shirt. The airport thermometer reads a mere sixty-eight degrees at this hour, but it feels extremely humid. I make haste, spending no more time than necessary alone in ladies room. Unfortunately, I'm on guard for all the horror stories I've heard about petty theft and muggings in Peru, most notably at airport and bus terminals. The scenarios range from outright assaults to very inventively choreographed distractions.

"Beware of the mustard scam," advised a well-meaning travel-tipster, "they'll smear you with mustard and while one person helps you clean it off, another is finding your wallet!"

"If you see a dollar bill lying on the sidewalk, don't pick it up," cautioned a travel agent, "It's all a setup to distract an unsuspecting tourist."

"Watch out for babies that are unexpectedly thrown into your arms."

"Replace your camera strap with a chain."

"Travel in groups at all times."

"Show no signs of affluence."

Casting further shadow is the fine print on a Travel Advisory pamphlet listing ominous forewarnings of fraudulent security police, abduction, bombings, strikes, landmines, carjacking, bandito taxi drivers, parasites, and even drug-infused chewing gum.

I come to Peru armed with warnings of all shapes and sizes, but mostly, I come with my dreams . . . and perhaps with a dose of such single-mindedness of thought as those tenacious predecessors who came before me.

2
THE FOUR CORNERS OF THE EARTH

Antonio Oliveras carries the white starched wedding dress of his niece, Leonora Maria de Sosa, who will be married tonight in the Church de la Merced in Cusco. Sitting directly across the aisle from me as my flight prepares for its landing, he beams a contagious widespread grin when he graciously invites me to both the wedding ceremony and the reception party, and of course, I accept.

Here at my window seat, a coveted position on the left side of the airplane, I turn to gape at the snow-capped Andes. Thanks to the efforts of an angel of sorts named Lourdes, whom I met while waiting in line at Lima airport this morning, I was assured my place. Torrential rains in Cusco caused yesterday's flights to be totally canceled, and as the backlog of frustrated passengers battled to be ticketed first, Lourdes, who identified herself as an unofficial tourist agent in Lima, fought to get me priority service. "You can put your trust in me," she said, and somehow, I believed her. Not that I have ever been one to place my trust so easily, at least not as a timorous child growing up in New York City. Yet here I was as an adult, roaming the globe from the time I earned my first paycheck. From the Mayan ruins of Chichen Itza to the vestiges of an ash-laden Pompeii, I had a special curiosity for archaeological sites and the mysteries of those lost peoples who inhabited them. How did such an apprehensive and fearful child grow up to become such a brazen world traveler, I often wondered. And where did this tenacity to foray the continents of the earth come from? Did my mind conjure puzzles of lost civilizations and then direct itself to solve them? And what was I really seeking to find in Peru?

From Lima to Cusco, we have quickly risen from sea level to 11,200 feet in the glorious Andes as our plane successfully touches ground at Velasco Asete Airport. It is forty-nine degrees here, with billowing popcorn-shaped clouds crisply outlined against an aqua blue sky. The surrounding turf is wet and green with a stripe of smoky white mist layered across the neighboring foothills. I say goodbye to the wide-eyed four-year-old sitting on my lap and return her to her rightful owner. Earlier, little Clara had scowled at me, crying floods of tears as she complained to her mother and the surrounding passengers that I had taken the window seat.

The onslaught of street-peddlers hawking souvenirs, hotels or a taxi ride for sale is unrelenting at Cusco's small airport terminal and it is surely a miracle when a well-appointed friend of Lourdes is able to find me in all the confusion. From out of the crowd, she heads right towards me. "My name is Mercedes," she announces. "Follow me." And from there it is all unremarkably straightforward, as she packs me off to an awaiting taxi and then disappears back into the crowd as quickly as she had materialized.

The Cusco city center is a mere five kilometers from the airport and it's only a matter of minutes before my taxi makes the segue from the industrial environs of airplane hangars and tarmac to the colorful perimeters of town. Designated in 1983 as a UNESCO World Heritage site in recognition of its cultural treasures, Cusco is an amalgam of the colonial and the indigenous, representing centuries of Inca and Quechua tradition infused with the influence of Spanish mores. Much like the western invaders who arrived on these shores hundreds of years ago, I enter as a fledgling and with equal fascination into an ancient world immortalized to the modern-day.

My mind snaps photos as flashes of impressions blink before my eyes. The cracked and peeling walls of adobe buildings are painted in all shades of pastel; powder blue, pink, saffron and eggshell. Cobble-stoned roads, slate grey and lumpy, rise and twist into snakelike labyrinths undecipherable to their destiny; while a Quechua woman leaves her long, heavy skirt swirling behind her in a blur of stripes as she disappears around the corner of a narrow, almost claustrophobic alley. At the core of city center, bustling street vendors fringe an arcaded promenade; manning canvas sacks and barrels from where breezy images of coca leaves and coffee beans, beaded necklaces and souvenirs, all flicker before my view. I spot the local cambio, pharmacia and trattoria, making a mental note of their location for future reference, as my taxi releases me to the gritty sidewalk curb at Calle Garcilaso.

I've chosen to stay at the Los Marqueses Residential, a three hundred year-old hacienda originally built for the Conquistador commandant Francisco Pizarro and subsequently converted into a monastery. Historical significance aside, its latest incarnation is as a reasonably priced pensione, just waiting for me to settle in. The fortress-like gateway fronting the sidewalk opens to the inner world of an arch-laden courtyard, steeped in the Spanish colonial style. Two levels of balcony are draped with pink and red fuchsia cascading from numerous clay pots and planters that edge a box-shaped garden where a large caged parrot stands guard. My room, which is quite modest at first glance, contains the bare necessities of a bed, nightstand and private bath, but is marked by the complexity of two ornately carved mahogany doors. Paired by elaborate brass handles and hinged with thick black, and apparently hand-tooled wrought iron, the magnificent portal speaks to a decadence befitting of an entrance of the onerous General Pizarro, himself.

A young Peruvian woman enters my room with a cup of tea, and in welcoming silence graced with a smile, motions to my head and stomach in an international sign language that tells me this is the notorious *maté de coca* that I've read about. Given almost immediately to travelers arriving at the sudden high altitude of 11,200 feet, coca leaves brewed in steaming hot water are said to alleviate the effects of *soroche*, otherwise known as high altitude sickness, and whose symptoms include headache, nausea and a feeling of suffocation. The coca plant is revered by Quechua natives, who chew its leaves along with a rind of lime, activating chemical properties that can add a feeling of fullness to their sometimes-empty stomachs. Indigenous to the local terrain of the highlands, these are the same coca leaves that are used to process cocaine. In their naturally harvested, then simple sun-dried form, the leaves of the coca plant can provide desensitization from the cold climate, as well as increased stamina during long hard hours of work. The habitual chewing of the leaves may even be responsible for the placid temperament of these descendants of the Inca, who by the face of it have seemingly achieved oblivion to the harsh conditions of high-altitude living.

I set out on foot to take a long walk, as is my custom the first day in a new city and am almost immediately struck by the overt presence of military force on the streets. Here in this once sacred place, the mythological center of the Inca Empire coined as the "Four Corners of the Earth" from-whence-all-things-came, stand triads of Peruvian militia armed with their machine guns as undisguised amongst street vendors and storefronts. The very fact that soldiers are stationed here speaks volumes of the uncertain conditions.

My first destination is the Plaza De Armas, just two blocks from my hotel. Here, I can get my bearings and take in the atmosphere around me. In old South America, the main plaza was the central hub of the city, and traditionally, the tallest and most important building, this being the main cathedral, was strategically located here. To the Spanish Conquistadores who conquered Peru, this well-planned positioning was no casual decision. The Baroque-style cathedral that now dominates the plaza was built upon the foundation of the former palace to the Inca god Viracocha, symbolizing to one and all the victory of the church over paganism. Combining the stonemasonry techniques of local Inca natives with the florid Renaissance design of the Spanish architect Juan Miguel de Veramendi, the impressive size of the cathedral, along with its looming bell tower and main altar exquisitely crafted in solid silver, would come to symbolize the autonomy of Spanish rule in Cusco.

Construction of the ornate basilica began in 1560 and continued for almost one hundred years until its completion. It is supplemented by two auxiliary houses of worship; the Church of El Triunfo (1536), and the Church of Jesus and Maria (1733). The huge cast iron bell that when it tolls may be heard from over forty kilometers away is more than two meters in height, and weighs in at over six tons. Named *Maria Angola* for the legendary Angolan slave who is said to have scattered gold dust in the iron as it was forged, the bell ranks as the largest of its kind in South America.

But long before the Spaniards fashioned this plaza to their tradition, there existed yet another hidden center here, whose clues are all around me if I know where to look for them. As the heart of the Inca Empire, this main plaza was once the anointed ground proclaimed by the Incas to be the "navel" of the earth from whence the very breath of life came. I seat myself on the edge of the cathedral steps and peruse the colonial arcades that rim the square, now housing cluttered souvenir shops and cafés. Then, I close my eyes and try to imagine another time long ago, before the Spanish invasion of 1532, when this very spot was deemed to be the holy center of the Inca Empire, designated by the honorific title of *Huacaypata*, "the place of joy."

The origin of the Inca civilization is a parable of mythology and historical data. Inca folklore tells a tale similar to that of Noah's Ark where in the aftermath of a catastrophic flood, the Supreme Creator Viracocha molded the first Incas, Manco Capac and his wife Mama Ocllo, from the clay of the submerged "Island of the Sun" (Isla Del Sol) on Lake Titicaca, the body of water between Bolivia and Peru. His divine act completed, it is said that Viracocha disappeared into a torrent of foam, never to be seen by human eyes again; hence the name Viracocha translates as "foam of the sea."

Recorded history tells us that the Inca civilization originated approximately 1200AD under the command of the legendary Sapa Inca (Sun King or Supreme Ruler) named Manco Capac. Inca society flourished for over three hundred years under a succession of rulers that included Pachacuti (1438-1471), Topa Inca (1471-1495) and Huayna Capac (1493-1525). Each new ruler of the empire declared their power by claiming to have been sent forth to earth directly by the Sun God Inti, the most important of the secondary deities to Viracocha and to whom all other Gods, *Pachamama* (Mother Earth), *Mamacocha* (Mother Sea), *Mamaquilla* (the Moon) and *Illapa* (Thunder and Lightning) were regarded as children or servants. In homage to the Sun God Inti, who provided the warmth and light essential to survival, Inca craftsmen fashioned precious objects of gold, creating a myriad of jewelry, ornaments, statues, and even gold-plated thrones and temples in the metal the Incas

9

dubbed "the sweat of the sun." During the Spanish conquest, the Incas would observe in perplexity the fervor with which the Conquistadores pilfered gold, thinking they either needed it to cure a strange disease, or surely must eat it.

The name "Peru" was totally unknown to the Incas, who referred to their empire imagistically as the "Four Quarters of the World" or *Tawantin-suyu,* comprising the quadrants *Chinchaysuyu, Antisuyu, Collasuyu,* and *Cuntisuyu.* With the city of Cusco (from the Quechua term *Qusqu,* sometimes seen spelled in the Colonial style as *Cuzco*) as the locus from which the borderlines of the quadrants radiated, Inca territories spread south to Chile and Bolivia and north to Colombia and Ecuador, covering an area over 2,500 miles long and two hundred miles wide. This was an empire four times the size of Egypt, boasting a population of over twelve million people. It was the largest commonwealth in pre-Columbian South America, comparable in reach to the power of ancient Rome.

As sophisticated architects, the Incas fashioned an infrastructure of highways, tunnels and suspension bridges, some of which are still in use today. Over ten thousand miles of road were paved from sea level to mountaintop, laced with more than one thousand *tambos,* the methodically placed shelters that doubled as rest-stops and supply stations, enabling an ingenious system of courier delivery across the territories of the vast domain. Designing cosmopolitan centers whose archaeological remnants display organization, purpose, and convenience, Inca stonemasons built palaces, forts, and residences that have endured centuries of earthquakes and weather.

The Incas were also expert farmers, developing terracing and irrigation systems to meet the challenges of the steep mountain slopes of the Andean range. Cultivating crops such as maize and potatoes in over two hundred assorted varieties, the Incas invented an advanced form of what we now refer to as a "freeze-drying" process, in order to conserve food supplies for the long winter months. These agricultural techniques were so well developed that it has led some anthropologists to speculate that the Inca culture may have derived from a more ancient peoples, perhaps thousands of years old.

When Francisco Pizarro and his army arrived in Peru, Cusco was the largest and wealthiest city in the South Americas. Unfortunately, by this time, the military law of "divide and conquer" had already been halfway accomplished by the Incas themselves, as Atahuallpa and Huascar, the sons of the Supreme Inca Huayna Capac, fought over succession to the royal throne. With the drowning of Huascar, as ordered by his brother Atahuallpa, conquest of the last royal was handily achieved. Mounted on horseback and fitted with the brute force of their steel weapons, Spanish soldiers captured Atahuallpa in an ambush at Cajamarca, to which his unarmed attendants were no match. It is astounding to consider in retrospect that the Inca Empire was conquered with little more than two hundred foot soldiers and a handful of horsemen armed with metal blades and guns. Were it not for the assistance of the disparate tribes of a civil war, who naïvely aligned themselves in confederation with Pizarro's troops, a united Inca front would surely have over-powered the Conquistadores and changed the course of history.

With that, the Spanish regime wasted no time in establishing a presence in its newly conquered territory. Heretofore, the term "Inca," which was once a title reserved exclusively for royalty, would be denigrated to a catch-all phrase describing the entire population of the highlanders. The redefined use of this moniker subsists to this day. Other transfigurations took more physical form. In the square where I now sit, remnants of Inca walls, once edifice for the grand palace of Viracocha were re-purposed to serve as the structural foundation for the main basilica that is the centerpiece of the plaza. To the south of me, the former "Temple of the Serpents," once the residence of the last Sapa Inca, Huayna Capac, has been supplanted by the colonial style Church De La Campania, built atop the ruins by Spanish architects. Just beyond it, the "House of the Chosen Women" (sometimes referred to as the House of the Virgins), where as many as 3,000 Inca women dedicated their lives to the Sun God Inti, has been displaced by the Convent of Santa

Catalina, a Spanish nunnery. The Baroque-style Church of Santo Domingo now occupies the former site of what was the most impressive of all Inca temples, the famed "Temple of the Sun" (also known as the *Coricancha*, from the Quechua term *Quri Kancha*, so-named for its Golden Courtyard). Here in this temple, walls posted with sheets of solid gold once adorned a huge core structure housing five sub-temples within it—all built in veneration to the Inca deities of nature; the Sun, Moon, Stars, Lightning and Rainbow. An enormous gold carving of the Sun God Inti was positioned at the nucleus of the temple, representing the source of all power. Rays of light, engraved in linear rows of gold, and studded with precious emeralds and jewels, emanated from the head of the Sun God in every direction. Facing east to receive the morning light, it must have been a grand sight to behold when the glimmering beams of the rising sun fell directly upon the temple each daybreak.

A wave of nausea lifts me from my daydream. Rippling its way across my unwilling stomach, I guess it to be the queasy flutters of a mild case of soroche. I reach into my vest pocket for one of the strategically placed Snickers bars that I carry with me when traveling to a foreign country, and take a bite. It has been my experience on many a traveler's journey that a tasty treat from home can become a scrumptious jewel in the desert when traversing distant lands; providing energy, and even psychological fortitude, when necessary. Besides the obvious physiological rise in sugar, the mental association to the memories of previous chocolate bars partaken of in homeland territory more familiar to the individual, may provoke a sense of comfort in the face of adversity. I stand up to clear my breathing path and take a few deep breaths to pull more oxygen into my lungs. A Quechua woman frying bread dough on the street corner looks at me knowingly. The rosy cheeks and robust chests of these natives, who are the closest descendants of the Incas, reflect a powerfully developed lung size and an increased red blood cell count evolved to breathe more easily in the rarified mountain air. As I am not so similarly endowed, I head to a local café.

"Are you an American?" Whether I asked the question or the question was asked of me, I do not recall, this being my introduction to Dirk, a tourist from Holland who would accompany me tonight to the wedding of Leanora Maria Sosa. Tall and lanky, with chin-length sandy brown hair and a Dutch/English accent characteristic of Europeans who have been schooled in the English language British-style, he easily invited himself to my table with his soft voice and friendly manner. A dairy farmer and café owner from the town of Edam (home of the cheese of same name), Dirk speaks four languages, owns a goat named Zyla, two cats, four cows, and a secret recipe for double-chocolate layer cake. Dirk has been in Cusco for five days and forewarns of a litany of obstacles ahead.

"The economy here is desperate . . . a time bomb."

"The newspapers are filled with reports of terrorists threats, especially to tourist attractions and government buildings."

"Guerillas have captured the hill town of Ayacucho." (Known for its multitude of churches, thirty-three of them to be exact, this was a place I had planned to visit.)

"Farmers are picketing the town square tomorrow."

"The railroad workers are on strike."

" . . . The train to Machu Picchu is not running."

My dreams are deflated with a word and the look on my face must have begged for the encouragement I needed because Dirk tries to recover his last statement by agreeing to help me inquire at the train station tomorrow morning.

I think to myself that there are never easy answers in a country like Peru where extremes of economic disparity between the rich and the poor create an impatience for change that cannot easily be met in quick time. The population of the highlands is ninety-nine percent native and one percent *mestizo* (mestizo being a combination of Spanish and native). Proud to have preserved the ancient Quechua language of the Incas (also commonly known as *Runasimi* or *mouth of the people*), these sole descendants of the Incas prefer to be called *natives* or *campesinos*, rather than *Indians*, which is considered to be an insult. In regional jargon, "Quechua" (warm valley people) or "Runa" (the people) is also appropriate.

13

It is only in the last few decades that Peruvian politicians began to acknowledge the influence of the Andeans and launched a campaign to appeal to their large numbers by proclaiming the ancient tongue of Quechua, which was formerly outlawed by the Spanish regime, as an official language. In 1970, under the rulership of President Juan Velasco, further advances were made when the face of the former Inca ruler, Tupac Amaru, began to appear on paper currency and land reforms transferred deeds from landlords back to the campesinos. However, in spite of these efforts, wages remained low in proportion to high profits grossed and living conditions for the highlanders showed little improvement. Ever leery of government officials, revolutionary groups such as the Sendero Luminoso (The Shining Path) and the Tupac Amaru Revolutionaries, began to form. The Sendero Luminoso, whose Marxist platform espouses self-determination of the commoners, emerged as the most significant of these organized groups, gaining attention by attacking government buildings, seizing small hill towns, and obstructing the tourist trade. In 1984, more than 6,000 government troops marshaled against the forces of the Sendero Luminoso. It is estimated that almost 3,000 people were killed, most of them poor peasants recruited from small villages in the mountains.

. . .

The Compari cocktails that Dirk and I order in the bar lounge of the high-priced hotel neither one of us is staying in, reminds Dirk that he once dreamed of owning a Compari Bar in Florence. This leads to a lengthy discussion about waking dreams and sleeping dreams, Aborigines, and all Peter Weir movies ever made—which diverts to a chain-link of conversation about Holland and Dirk's café, Edam and Edam cheese, books, cars, Malibu and Monterey. I take notice that Dirk is on his third drink.

Perhaps because I am a stranger and there is little chance that I will divulge particulars to anyone of consequence in his life, Dirk confides to me a deeply personal regret. "I should have warned him not to fly that night," he blurts, speaking of the anguished, disturbing dreams that plagued him, both before and after his young brother's untimely death. "I should have followed my instincts and told him not to go." Leaning back in his chair with shoulders slumped downwards; his body language could be translated as fatigue, were it not for the pained look of self-defeat seeping from his eyes. There is an uneasy lapse of silence in which the weight of Dirk's words is awkwardly suspended in mid-air. "You must have loved your brother very much," I say.

I have frequently been the recipient of confidences from travelers on the road, and always, I am taken aback by the sense of self-abandonment that occurs when we are removed from our daily environment and discover the newfound ability to say what we will without repercussion. When we travel, we are without a history in the eyes of others. We travel in ambiguity of a biography, without the luggage of a backstory apart from that which we choose to reveal. When we are a traveler, there is no judgment or blame to be assigned, no comparison that can be made alongside our peers, and no real knowledge of what is true about us.

Travelers that I have encountered in passing have revealed to me the startling privacies of their fatal illnesses, deformities, unlawful acts, and sufferings of loss by death or betrayal. Perhaps they yearn to be relieved of a heavy burden, purged of some long-held guilt, or desire to find that we too, have experienced the same sorrow. Traveling affords us the opportunity to enjoy safety in anonymity. Through the short-lived relationships we share with persons we most likely shall never see again, we find a foil against which we can test for a reaction—or discover the courage to ask a question that we ordinarily would never have the nerve to ask. By way of journey, the traveler comes to live in the sequestered state of an interim period of movement; in transit between the life left behind and the life that will be returned to. Temporarily without a past, and with a future as merely as consequential as the next train or plane one catches, the space of the unfamiliar serves to liberate us as we travel, encouraging a shedding of inhibition and a release from those constraints that would otherwise bind us when in familiar territory. Travel opens, and that opening makes us less guarded, less fixed in our habits, and less of our old selves. In this way, we are free, or freer when we are a traveler.

The wedding of Leanora and Roberto took place promptly at 7:30pm in the Church de la Merced in Cusco, attended by family, friends and invited tourists. With stalwart chest and head held high, Antonio Oliveras was transformed from the airline passenger across the row from me to a very earnest-looking uncle who proudly led his niece down the aisle. The wedding dress that Antonio had so carefully carried over his arm all the way from Lima, now bedecked the beautiful bride, eliciting smiles and sighs from all who viewed her. The miniature wedding favor gifted to me was a tiny crocheted basket, hooked with a tag that read *Leanora y Roberto Aguilar*. Dirk's momento was an American cigarette, humorously adorned with a top hat and coat. I'll admit to keeping my ball of rice as a souvenir, instead of throwing it at the bride and groom.

3
THE JAW OF THE PUMA

I never snapped her photo, but I can still see her face in my mind's eye; this being the beautiful Quechua woman whom we stopped to speak with today at the crest of the hill leading to Sacsayhuaman. Following a quick breakfast and a brief inquiry at the train station, Dirk and I decide to visit the ruins of the Inca fortress on the north end of Cusco, phonetically pronounced as *Sox-say-why-mahn* and translating into English as *Royal Hawk*. The railroad workers are still on strike and there are no connections at all to Machu Picchu today.

The steep climb along the craggy cobblestone hill of Calle Suecia is a forty-minute hike, including my numerous rest stops along the way. Dirk, who has been in Cusco for five days, is already acclimatized to the low oxygen content of the air and I am moving at a feverish pace to keep up with him. So steep is the approach to Sacsayhuaman from this end of town that the Incas deemed it inaccessible to their enemies, defending it with only one wall. From my personal experience, I can now understand why, as I imagine dozens of Conquistadores, dressed in the weight of their full armor, pausing to gasp for breath, just as I do.

Shooting no photographs on my laborious climb, I use my eyes and full attention to capture moments as I pass the numerous iron-gated courtyards facing onto the street and offering privileged glimpses into the everyday lives of those inhabitants who reside inside. Gardens, candle-lit altars of devotion, naïve wall paintings, and even the ordinary sight of a woman hanging laundry become a source of fascination to me. Just ahead, a small child, who could be no more than four years of age, squeals in victorious delight as she hauls off a scrap of corrugated tin (surely a foot larger than herself), as if a prized possession. Two tan-skinned and spindly limbed adolescent boys race each other to the corner, then collapse in fits of laughter on the hot, sullied pavement. And beyond the rising knoll, the striking contour of a llama, dramatically silhouetted against the morning sun, is poised at the horizon.

Never knowing what delicious sights he has missed, Dirk awaits at the threshold of Sacsayhuaman, where three Quechua women are leading their llamas alongside the entrance. Dressed in the traditional garb characteristic to the indigenous natives, their bolero-style jackets and bowler hats are embroidered in the brightly colored hues of the rainbow. One of the women steps forward in curiosity. She hesitates, and then squints, as if attempting to examine me more closely. Graced with the full round face of her ancestors that is strikingly reminiscent of North American Eskimo or Tibetan features, her raven black hair falls in two thick braids, all the way down to her waist. I think to myself that the solemnity of her dignified expression must surely mask some ancient secret of the motherland.

"Mo-mune-yay, mo-mune-yay," the Quechua woman twice repeats, in a whisper barely audible to my ear. She motions to a plant off the side of the road and picks off one of its transparent green leaves, holding it up to the sun. "Muña," she explains to us in simple Spanish, is a natural wild herb whose fragrance brings relief from high altitude sickness, which by the look of us, she must be fairly certain we are suffering from. I gesture a nod of understanding and break a leaf to inhale its sweet sage aroma. Dirk, who has meanwhile been inspired to investigate the bush, thinks he has spotted the medicinal herb nicknamed "Tres Gatos" (Three Cats), a purple flower that is easily recognizable for its bloom resembling three catheads with pointed ears. He confirms his find with the Quechua woman, then snaps off a sprig and hands it to me.

Peru is one of the most bio-diverse countries in the world, with an ecosystem that is home to over 25,000 species of plants. The feral shrubs and herbs that grow in abundance in these mountains serve as an important resource for isolated populations lacking access to healthcare, and have provided curative powers to the Quechua for many centuries. Some plant species found here are known for the inducement of visions, such as the tall columnar cactus, the *Trichocereus Pachanoi* (in Runa called *Wachum*). Notable for the potency of its hallucinogenic properties, this native plant is regarded by local shamans as "the keeper of the keys to heaven" and is a source of curiosity for travelers seeking altered experiences.

The line drawing of a puma in my Peruvian guidebook depicts the layout of the city of Cusco, as designed by Inca architects. Clearly, Sacsayhuaman represents the head of the puma, an animal revered by the Andeans for its strength and elusiveness to capture. Each of the three walls of the immense stone fortress measures over one thousand feet in length, running parallel to each other in a triple-protective stance. Juxtaposing each other in a zigzag configuration, perhaps these walls were meant to symbolize the fierce teeth of the feline, faced away from the city in a defensive posture aimed at its enemies.

Without the use of the wheel, these massive stones, some of them weighing a mind-boggling three hundred tons, were cut from a quarry over a mile away and then transported to this site. How did the Incas move these enormous boulders into position, one over the other? And even more bewildering, how did they carve them to fit so precisely, each as a puzzle piece meeting its part? It is famously noted that with no mortar or adhesive whatsoever, the placement of the boulders is so exacting that even a razor blade cannot fit between them. This achievement of craft has baffled even the most educated of observers. As a stone carver myself, I try to reach into the mind of the Inca. Having seen Michelangelo's La Pieta (and Sistine Chapel, for that matter) with my own eyes, I do believe that a deep one-pointedness of mind incurred by the devotion of art to a sense of religiosity renders seemingly impossible feats, possible. This has proven so in ancient cultures throughout the ages, where dedication to belief of a greater good (usually manifesting in a combination of the empire and the divine), could literally move mountains both physical and non-physical, resulting for example, in mammoth accomplishments such as the Great Pyramids of Egypt. Story has it that the Incas sang songs as they built their fortress walls and temples, chanting uplifting lyrics to the Sun God Inti as they toiled. So infectious were these melodic tunes that the Spaniards

19

themselves adapted much of the music for their own entertainment. Based on this conjecture, it is entirely reasonable to me that the combination of the unifying power of song, the strength of inspiration, and the simple tenacity of the laborer's hard work, made the construction of these walls possible.

A tour group hovers nearby and I overhear the tour guide recount a trendy pop-culture theory that attributes the construction of Sacsayhuaman to interplanetary aliens who landed in Peru on UFOs to help the Incas build their kingdom. What the tour guide fails to consider is what a great insult this is to the Quechua natives, a proud people who feel this as yet another attempt to rob them of the achievements of their Inca heritage.

At one time, three round towers are legended to have stood ground here at the site of Sacsayhuaman; one of them rising over five stories tall. It is logical that they likely served as lookout points of some kind. The towers, if they ever existed, were most probably dismantled by the Spaniards, who used the valuable stones to build their cathedral and residences. What lofty towers might once have been, are now relegated to the realm of folklore, with no traceable remnants to be evidenced today. Surviving the pillage remains what appears to be a large throne chiseled from a single piece of granite. One may imagine a time when the reigning Sapa Inca sat upon this very throne and observed his troops parading by in their full regalia at the annual "Inti Rayma" (*Festival of the Sun*) held here each June at Summer Solstice.

The fortress walls become fodder for my camera, as I zoom in on the most uncanny of the carved stones with impossible angles resting one upon the other. Asking permission first, I photograph a little Quechua girl whose mother offers to iron my wrinkled shirt— and in an instant I am catapulted into the self-conscious world of what I am wearing, which is evidently wrinkled. Soon, I am surrounded by six or seven vendors selling jewelry, and purchase a handful of beaded necklaces in vibrant colors. Each of the clay beads strung to the necklace has been individually rolled, fired, and hand-painted with figures of tiny black llamas set against a flurry of fuschia and green paint. These beautiful necklaces are unique, one-of-a-kind art pieces, yet they cost the equivalent of a trifling fifty cents. In a reverse system of values that reveals the polarity of sophistication between the isolated hill towns and the industrialized cities, machine-made products off a production line are esteemed to be of more worth than the rough-hewn items individually wrought by hand.

Dirk disappears to go rock hunting and I stroll to the amphitheater at the edge of the ruin site. I rest on an incline and soak in the sky, the clouds, the view of the city below, and the magnificent ramparts of Sacsayhuaman. Falling into a meditative spell, I watch in stillness as a docile herd of llama goes home for the day; each one of them lined up perfectly one behind the other and going to I-don't-know-where. As a descendant of the camel, this species of llama is reputed to have crossed the Bering Straits into the Americas during the great Ice Age and for the campesinos of the Andes is primarily useful as a beast of burden, with the capacity to carry small loads of up to one hundred pounds. Its cousins, the alpaca, the vicuna, and the guanacos are often confused with the llama and are rather preferred for their fine wool, which is warmer and lighter than that of the sheep. Nicknamed *Faithful Brother*, the domesticated llama is easily trained to obey the voice of its master and makes a fine and loyal companion. With its furry white coat, long willowy neck, and delicacy of movement, the llama brings the word *graceful* to mind. Sitting at my spot on the hill, I am somewhat transfixed by the sight of them—and I hold my gaze steadily until they disappear beyond the ridge.

• • •

The Museum of Archaeology is closed for the second day in a row. Both Dirk and I have been rapping on its doors to no avail, ever since we arrived in Cusco. We have each, in our independent research, read of the treasure of artifacts the museum houses and were looking forward to seeing the numerous hand tools, textiles, pottery, and most importantly, the Inca mummies unearthed from local ruins. However, despite the sign on the door, which clearly states that the museum is open Monday through Saturday, neither of us has had any luck getting in. Hearing the rising chants of demonstrators resounding from the Plaza De Armas, I have to wonder if the museum workers are also on strike.

"Hasn't been open in weeks," I hear a voice say. "And pay no attention to the sign on the door. You are on *hora peruana*, that's Peruvian time here."

The man behind the voice is Richard, an American anthropologist from Florida. The rumpled khaki hat drawn tightly over his forehead is evocative of an Indiana Jones swashbuckler, made more convincing by his penetrating eyes and deliberate swagger. The appendage of a leather bomber jacket completes the full ensemble of what I would easily believe is a charismatic adventurist setting out on an archaeological dig of some excitement. Richard has been living in Cusco for the past year, courtesy of a grant that affords him the opportunity to repair the erosion of Inca terraces in the Sacred Valley. A lover of South America, he has previously spent fourteen years in the Galapagos Islands, and from all appearances is delighted to come upon some Westerners from the States. Over a superb dinner of *sopa con pan* and *pescado con papas fritas*, Dirk and I are all ears as Richard gives us the lowdown on the current situation in Cusco.

"The campesinos who pick the coca leaves are on strike. They are paid a pittance, in spite of the fact that there is a tremendous profit from the sale of the leaves. To put it simply the campesinos want more money—and they want it now," says Richard, removing his hat and propping it on the table for emphasis. "The tension is building to a breaking point. Yesterday, a shipment of coca came in from Puno. The bales were unloaded, and then burned in protest. This was a very bold and defiant move."

"And the military," I interject, "I see them everywhere, even on rooftops, armed with their rifles."

"If you had been here two weeks ago, you would have seen a tank positioned right in the middle of the plaza," says Richard, arching his eyebrows. "It was a military show of force. The government doesn't need any more trouble here—not on top of all the threats from the Sendero Luminoso."

"What about the trains to Machu Picchu?" I ask. "I came all the way here to see Machu Picchu. How will I get there?"

"The train workers are striking in sympathy with the farmers. They know that when tourist dollars are at stake, this puts the pressure on. But it will all come to a head in ten days or so," Richard underscores, "when Halley's Comet makes its grand appearance—that's when tourists will be packing in by the busloads and one side or the other will be forced to capitulate. I'd recommend you continue on your tour of Peru and then come back later when all this levels down."

That Halley's Comet could indirectly have an effect on the actions of the people is, in some ways, not dissimilar to ancient societies that may have modified their behavior upon its arrival. So why such a fuss over Halley's Comet at this time and this place? The fact is, that this most celebrated of comets, first assessed for its reliable return by the British astronomer Edmond Halley (1656-1742), affords us the rare opportunity to see a comet in our lifetime. Most comets traversing the celestial heavens may visit the region of earth's solar system only once every thousands of years. But Halley's Comet, one of about a hundred "short-term" comets known to humankind, takes its predictable course approximately every seventy-six years, lured in by the gravitational pull of our fringe planets and coming close enough to earth to be visible to the naked eye. This prehistoric ball of ice, the residue of the formation of the universe, is currently on its outward journey, headed back into the nebulous expanse of outer space for another seventy-six years. As it makes this final orbit, the comet passes low in the sky, and is best seen from the Southern Hemisphere of earth, where by serendipity, I currently stand.

I quietly mull over Richard's suggestion. I have certainly planned to explore other areas of Peru and have even considered taking a bus to Arequipa to see the famous lines of Nazca. But that would entail the Pan American Highway, of which wary travelers have advised me is often washed out and unreliable. I consider that I could fly directly to Arequipa or even catch a flight to La Paz in neighboring Bolivia, then circle my way back overland to Peru.

Richard, in the laid-back manner of his southern tropical homeland, assures me that it will all work out. "Don't worry, I know you'll find your way."

These words reverberate in my mind. It seems to me that the traveler's path is often a crooked one, whose detours comprise a unique fashioning that we may only understand when looking back in retrospect. This morning, as we were trying to decipher the shape of the puma's jaw as outlined by the fortress at Sacsayhuaman, I couldn't help but think of the Danish writer Isak Dinesen (*aka Karen Blixen*) in her recounting of "The Roads Of Life,"[2] a childhood tale she was read aloud with moving pictures as a child. As the story goes, a young man is awakened from his sleep in the middle of the night by an awful noise and then sets forth from his bed to find its source. From north to south and east to west in all directions he searches, stumbling over boulders and falling into ditches at every misread turn. Despite his cuts and bruises, and undaunted by the obstacles he meets, the man continues his quest into the night, up one path and then another, falling down and getting up again, slipping into mud holes, then climbing out. With each new attempt, he is entirely confident that he has finally discovered the origin of the vexing noise, only to be proven wrong once more. By way of story, we may admire this person for the bullish fervor with which he persists in his search for the origin of the sound from every conceivable vantage point. The metaphor of the falling and rising in and out of one ditch and then another may be analogized to the missteps and trials of life. Sometimes, we are so sure that we are on the right track and following the true course to which we are called, only to be felled and then pressed to try again. However, just as in the story of "The Roads of Life," what the frustrated man cannot see from his subjective position is that the tracings of his footsteps are beginning to take on a shape. Indeed, when darkness lifts to morning, the man is confounded by the image of a stork spread out before him in the garden. Made apparent by light of day, his numerous gaffes and falls have created the distinctive outline of a long-legged stork, the figure of which could not have been made in any other way.

Karen Blixen kept this story close to her heart in time of need to remind herself that we cannot always see the reason for the circumstance we are presently in, but must have confidence that we will come to understand its greater meaning at a later time. The tale of the stork echoed as I stood at the jaw of the puma at Sacsayhuaman today.

4

THE EARTH SHAKER & THE PARTRIDGE BIRD

Pachachuti, or *Earth Shaker* is a Runasimi term referencing an apocalypse, a cataclysm, or a world in reversal. It is a turn of phrase sometimes used by the Andeans to describe the upheaval of a catastrophic earthquake, wherein the world as it was previously known is turned upside-down. It is also an expression that would aptly describe the state of the Inca Empire after the Spanish invasion of 1532. With one world torn apart and another reconstituted upon it, the past would now lie beside the present in the deep sleep of surrender; its holy remnants obscured by shadow.

To this end, the Quechua view history as divided into two ages; the Age of the Ancients and the Age of the Christians. In the aftermath of the Spanish conquest, worship of the Sun God Inti and other deities of nature were strictly forbidden. With royal Inca leaders annihilated or rendered impotent, a concerted effort took place to eradicate pagan tenets and impart Christian ideology upon the masses. From the stones of ransacked palaces and temples, the churches of Christianity would now stand poised upon the ruins of formerly sacred Inca sites, where crucifixes and statues of saints displaced the idols of paganism. A new page had been turned. The cataclysm had occurred. For the Incas, the world was in reversal, with no turning back.

With the passing of time, Inca traditions began to fade in memory and as new generations were born into a Spanish dominated culture, the finer details of Inca credo would be lost forever. This was most especially due to the fact that the Incas kept no written record of their illustrious empire. Up until this time, the Inca's transmittal of knowledge had been almost entirely dependent on the oral tradition of storytelling, song, and the use of an original device called a *Quipu*. Translated in English as *knot*, the Quipu was a device composed of colored threads twisted together to form a primary rope about two feet long, from which hung a number of shorter cords in varying sizes and colors tied with strategically placed knots. In a mathematical system reminiscent of the abacus, the distance between the knots and the color and position of the threads appear to represent numerical quantifications. Perhaps the spacing at intervals along the knots designated decimal points or arithmetic computations of some kind, but no one can be sure of this.

Quipus of varying length and complexity were translated by "Quipucamayocs" (or *Keepers of the Quipu*), who were the record-keepers of their day. It is believed that this system of knots was the manner by which the Incas maintained archives of births, deaths, weaponry, grain, and perhaps even the positions of the sun and moon. Those called "Rememberers" used the Quipu as a catalyst to tell stories, with each knot aiding the memory by way of association. Extending the Quipu at a full arms length, Rememberers had only to see the color and twist of a knot in order to recall sentimental stories of the great Sapa Incas, important historical events, and the mythological tales of creation to be transmitted through generations. This ingenious method of oral tradition prevailed as a means of passing down knowledge in the same spirit as did the ancient storytellers of the Celts and the Greeks. Based upon this practice and the inference of the moniker assigned to its narrators as "Rememberers," it is conjectured that the Inca possessed a heightened capacity for memory, displaying a retentive brainpower that reached far back into the annals of history. One may imagine the centuries of knowledge held within whole thoughts, as represented by a single colored knot.

Some critics have pointed to the absence of the written word as a lack of acuity on the part of the Incas, nonetheless, it is generally understood that oral cultures are characterized by a strong identification with nature, and thus, have no necessity for symbolic demarcation. In fact, the lack of hieroglyphics may actually enhance our understanding of the Incas' potent relationship with the natural world. The fact that the Incas kept no written records might also have been augmented by intentional purposes of secrecy. After all, how difficult can it be to scratch a circle on a stone and agree that it will represent the sun, for example? Certainly, the Incas were intelligent enough to figure that out. I myself, am skeptical of the analysts who treat this issue, along with the apparent absence of the wheel in Inca society, as a deficiency. Perhaps, the real question to ponder is: Did the Incas keep no written records because they *couldn't*—or because they *wouldn't*? Remains of Quipus may be found in the local museum at Cusco, but unfortunately, the art of reading the Quipu, has been totally lost. Along with other unresolved mysteries of Inca stonework, vessels, and art, its true purpose is an enigma.

It is with thanks to the efforts of Felipe Waman Puma, a 16th century writer and illustrator, that some characteristics of Inca dress and ceremony have been chronicled. Descriptions by the Conquistadores themselves, who translated the Quechua language into the Roman alphabet, also spread information by letters and word of mouth. The most notable of these historical records is "The Royal Commentaries of the Incas," the romanticized journals of Garcilaso de la Vega, a mestizo whose mother was an Inca princess. Today, most Quechua natives, as the last descendants of the Incas, are devout Catholics. What ancient myth and imagery of the Inca civilization that has endured the passage of time has been integrated into the culture. Although somewhat homogenized by their journey, these traditions remain important to religious observance and faith.

In such an example, the crucifix of "El Senor de las Temblores" (The Lord of the Earthquakes) in the Church de La Compagna in Cusco draws pilgrims from all of Peru. Perhaps speaking to the struggling lives of its residents, the blackened Christ figure hanging from the cross is a more agonized representation of pain than those found on crucifixes of devotion in Euro-Western cultures. This is a Christ figure whose wounds are deeper and bloodier, with a dramatically tortured body that writhes in torment from its binds. He is a Christ figure whose suffering may be mirrored in the hearts of the Andeans, as they offer prayers for safety from the apocalypse of the great Pachachuti, *The Earth Shaker*.

. . .

It was one of those Cusco mornings when the mountains met the clouds. The air that had once stole my breath, now exhilarated me. During our breakfast of watermelon juice and pancakes with sliced bananas that tasted more like kiwis than bananas, Dirk and I agree to accompany each other on an excursion to Ollantaytambo in The Sacred Valley. A small village about 85 kilometers from Cusco, the magnificent fortress at Ollantaytambo was one of the last Inca strongholds against the Spaniards, and was the site of a battle between the armies of Hernando Pizarro and the Sapa Inca, Manco II.

Our small white van, packed tight with eight other sightseers, trollops over the undulating road like a roller coaster losing and gaining speed at the heights and depths of its curvatures. The view from my window parallels a vast expanse of soft rolling hills, patched in every shade of green imaginable and stepped with the flawless boxed lines of Inca terraces that stretch before us in all their harmony of uniformity and order. A transparent veil of cloud vapor crowns the precipitous slopes, with always, the towering Andes looming overhead, ever in their watchful state.

Back in Los Angeles, just a few days before my departure for Peru, I had gazed up at the foothills northwest of the city, while stopped at a traffic light. Over the clatter of motorcars, honking horns and impatient drivers, I focused my eyes above the urban scene that enveloped me to a bare area of the hillside up ahead. A lovely white mist was rising over the crest of the hill; gently floating in the cast of an afternoon sky. For a few brief moments, my imagination shifted to another location. If I were to avoid lowering my line of vision to the traffic in front of me, and rather instead fix my gaze upon the hill . . . was this Peru? Now, with the very same pointedness of a fixed stare lifted upwards, but this time from the window of a tiny white van, I spy a white haze rising with ghost-like delicacy over the foothills of the Andean range. The vista is a flashback to that moment stopped in traffic, and for a brief instant, my mind does not distinguish between the two experiences.

A rest-stop at Pisac (*Pisaq*), a small brown village of adobe and stone about twenty-five miles into our journey, offers us the opportunity to shop at the local Indian market. Named for the partridge bird, Pisac was an otherwise tranquil community until the rackety engine of our motorcar invaded its calm. Were it a Thursday or a Sunday, these cobbled streets would be thick with the clamor of commerce, but today is not a designated market day in Pisac, and it looks as if only a handful of vendors have set up their stalls just beyond the square.

I spot a stray cow, and then a solitary pig, straddling the path of an oh-so-narrow alleyway, as if on their way to a very important event. They join together in the open round of the village center and mix freely among a small group of curious children gathering around our van. "Allillanchu mama? Allillanchu?" (*How are you, madam, how are you?*) the children demand to know. It appears that we are the major event in town, at present. Surrounded by a pig, a cow and a dozen children all vying for my attention, I notice one small child in particular, who is set apart from the crowd by standing shyly in the background. About five years of age, and of the sweetest disposition, she coyly sneaks glances at me, the foreign stranger in her American blue jeans. Dressed in a crimson and yellow-striped dress that is somewhat tattered at the edges, the little girl carries what must be her baby brother slung papoose-style over her back, bearing her child-caring task as if in the utmost natural course of things. Most probably this child is babysitting her younger sibling while her mother tends to a nearby merchant booth. I gesture to my camera and ask permission to snap a photo, all the while thinking how enormous her eyes are; so deep a chocolate brown and so busy in their probing. As I head off for the marketplace, I consider that the few cents I have paid her are inequitable in view of the fact that I will have such a priceless memory for life.

At the Indian Market, Dirk is hustling like a pro. "I'm only a poor Dutchman," he says, unabashedly pleading his case and bargaining for every last cent. Lacking in the skill of negotiation, I defer after only one-round of banter, purchasing my first alpaca sweater of a brown and white geometric design. Never having been very good at the bargaining process, I pay way too much for it, and then fall victim to an overzealous salesman who convinces me to buy a lovely looking poncho, which I will later find out is made of polyester. Beckoned by an Inca Kola sign (*Inka Cola* is a very sweet Peruvian soda), it is with great reticence that I enter through a doorway that leads to what looks more like someone's kitchen than a restaurant (it probably was someone's kitchen) and quench my high altitude thirst with the extremely sweet soda pop. The empty bottle makes a great souvenir, and I stow one away in my tote bag.

Soon, passengers begin boarding the van to resume our journey, but the Inca terraces above the cliffs overlooking Pisac distract me. Their dominating presence cannot be denied, and I'm aware of the extraordinary ruins that reside just an hour's hike behind them. I wander off in their direction, as if called by the remnants I cannot see and risking being left behind as once happened to me at the Oracle of Delphi in Greece.

"Hurry up," Dirk hollers, "you'll miss the bus!"

5

TIME IS A ROOM

The roar of the war cry echoed from the living rock like a thunder exploding across the sky. Huge boulders, studded in sharp thorny edges, headed down the embankment on a death roll destined towards the approaching enemy. This time, the Royal Inca rode on horseback, leading his fearless warriors in a barrage of javelins, arrows and hand-wrought missiles. He was adorned in the full plumage of his imperial ancestry; the crimson borla around his forehead, the golden ornaments in his hair, and the metal breastplate that shielded him embellished with sparkling jewels, bespeaking his Inca sovereignty. Twice, the Spanish soldiers retreated in order to regroup, and twice they were forced to withdraw, unable to withstand the aggressive onslaught. This triumphant tour de force was the last great victory of the Inca in a battle led by Manco II, here, at the extraordinary fortress at Ollantaytambo.

From the heights of Cusco, we have descended to an altitude of 9,200 feet above sea level in the Sacred Valley. As we enter the small village of Ollantaytambo, our bus moves cautiously, as if barely able to squeeze through the cramped, narrow streets. In fact, the adobe houses lining our pathway are so close that I almost feel as if I could stretch my arm out the window of the van to touch their walls. It is the awkward circumstance I find myself in that my elevated seat on the bus positions me as yet one more invader of this land—this time in the guise of a tourist staring directly into the faces of the Quechua women who pause to look up from their chores, as we, the intruders, leer only inches away.

The historic village of Ollantaytambo is situated directly below the central fortress and contains many original Inca residences characterized by their finely carved stone walls, once-existent thatched roofs, and shared yards. The blueprint of the city is classic

Inca layout, typified by a main plaza, a sundial, an outpost, a central palace, a requisite House of the Chosen Women, and of course, the great *pucará* (fortress) we have come to inspect. This is a magnificent cityscape to behold—and one certainly gets the impression that Inca nobles must have resided here.

Unlike the rows of defensive walls at Sacsayhuaman, the fortress of Ollantaytambo, which was still a work in progress when abandoned, is built in the likeness of an open amphitheater with only one perimeter wall defending it. Arranged in the configuration of a steep grade of terraces, its long flat steps rise in height to the brow of the mountain, where a pair of watchtowers positioned on either side of the horseshoe serve as lookout points to detect the approaching enemy. This strategic positioning served as a brilliant defensive posture, utilizing and building upon the natural assets of the terrain in that it would take the oncoming adversary a good length of time to climb the terraces, thereby rendering them as open targets to the blitz of projectiles spiraling towards them. The landscape setting provides additional safeguarding with one side of the concave-designed fortress facing the Lares Valley, and the backside of it forming an almost sheer cliff with a deadly drop to the raging rapids of the Urumbamba River below.

I climb all the way to the uppermost landing where a religious monument of peculiar form looms above us, defiant to all reason. "I don't believe it!" Back in Cusco, I had chuckled to myself when I heard a tourist speak those words. He was viewing a solitary stone carved in ten-angled edges fixed around a doorway without a single break in the granite. His comment had not been voiced in a tone of awe and wonder, but in a "no-I-don't-believe-it-they-have-got-to-be-kidding" manner. Now, as I gawk at the titanic stone columns towering before me, I find myself muttering, "How can this be?" Popularly known as the *Wall of Six Monoliths*, this manmade phenomenon is composed of six rectangular blocks, each of them approximately thirteen feet high and six feet wide and estimated to individually weigh fifteen tons apiece. Between each of the six pillars, a tapered slice of granite functions as either decoration or filler, complementing its neighboring block with the utmost of precision. It is unfathomable that these huge boulders could have been carried to this position from the quarry below—and then their hard surface carved in such a perfectly smooth, flat fit. How did they do it? In my mind, I envisage a theory whereby the Incas never carved the stones at all, but perhaps with the aid of heat, water and chisel, split the slabs in the manner of hacking firewood with an axe, then puzzled the fragments back together for the consummate fit. This logic is illogical, of course, because what force of power could have accomplished such a feat? The mass tonnage I see before me— impossible! Were crane-like devices used to crash boulder upon boulder, rupturing the granite so that the pieces were easier to move . . . then their edges rasped and rejoined? Even Hiram Bingham, who conducted numerous investigations into the mind-boggling accomplishments of Inca architects, never found evidence of crane-like devices, but speculated that rollers or levers made of bronze could have been used to move the boulders. However, this theory cannot explain the Herculean lifting of mass tonnage, nor the level plane of the perfectly smooth veneer. Along with a small group of other awe-struck sightseers, I hypothesize possibilities until my exhausted brain signals me to stop thinking so hard. I let it go and surrender. I am content to remain at wonder with the rest.

. . .

It was raining again and the grass was greener than green. The air felt close and full, permeated with that fresh feeling one gets when standing by the sea; the atmosphere thick with the richness of water. To the Incas, everything was alive and imbedded with soul; human, animal, plant, mountain and rock. This would mean that the very stones used to build Inca monuments were composed of the same sacred spirit as all humans. The concept of heaven and earth were not viewed as two separate realms, but as existing simultaneously as one reality on three levels: "Hanaq Pacha," *the upper world or heaven*; "Kay Pacha," *this world*; and "Ukhu Pacha," *the inner world or underworld*. The notion of what Judeo and Christian traditions call heaven or paradise, as a place of spirit was as real and tangible as the ground itself, with no division between. For the Incas, divinity was close at hand in the here-and-now, with no passage of time, suffering, or death incurred to reach it.

"Time is not just a road, it's also a room," said the novelist John Fowles. Indeed, time is not merely a course of direction, nor a passage of years, but a storehouse of detail cached within the boundary of our minds. The room of time may be a metaphor for the space of memory, with the walls around it and the contents within (both visible and invisible) sometimes embodied in the semblance of a city street, a warm kitchen, a smiling face, or an unseen thought. So it is here, at the great pucará at Ollantaytambo where I am surrounded by the walls of circumstance and time. If I listen closely, I can still hear the war cries, I can still hear the wails. Here on this ground, I stand in memory among the ghosts of Inca warriors, who held in their hands the very survival of their civilization as a delicate piece of china, soon to be shattered and lost forever.

Victory at Ollantaytambo was to be short-lived for the Inca. After having successfully held back the Conquistadores on two separate occasions, Manco II, brother of the tragically drowned King Huascar, was to suffer a crushing defeat. Dizzy with the drink of *chicha*, the fermented beer extracted from the sap of the maize stalk, Inca guardians of the fortress were duped by a surprise raid and overwhelmed by Spanish forces. Helpless to prevent his son (the heir apparent to the throne) from capture by the enemy, Manco II and his attendants fled deep into the jungles between the Urubamba and Apurimac Rivers to the refuge called Vilcabamba. In this remote sanctuary, whose exact location is still a controversy to this day, Manco II would live in hiding well into the year of 1532, sheltered by an obstacle course of raging rapids, insurmountable mountain passes and sheer cliff. If at first, the Incas had naïvely believed that the Conquistadores held the power of lightning in their steel guns and had been sent to them by the Creator-God Viracocha—they did not believe it now. The Conquistadores had proven themselves to be otherwise barbarous. With their callous acts of pillage, murder, and broken promises, they came to represent the greatest of all evil symbols to the Inca—that of "Supay"—*the Devil*.

Theory abounds, that Ollantaytambo, the place once called *Tampu*, was more than just a simple village with a fortress where a great battle took place, but also a burial ground and hamlet of procreation. The journals of Garcilaso de la Vega suggest the presence of holy caves where the entrails of deceased Inca royals may have been hidden. Quechua legend mythologizes that the first Inca, Manco Capac, and his sister/wife Mama Ocllo, settled here in Tampu and procreation what was to become the entire Inca population. Indeed, it seems a special locale, a place of power and significance, evidenced by the visceral feeling that moves through one's body, just by being here.

On the descent from the fortress, Dirk and I stop to converse with an Inca child whom we have noticed sitting in the rain for the entire day, perched on a step of Inca terrace and dressed in the full costume of her Quechua ancestry. She is a vision in her red saucer-shaped hat and hand-sewn cape embroidered with the multi-colored threads of triangular patterning that is prototypical of the Inca style. The little girl tugs at her dirty torn slip of a dress, pulling it tautly over her knees as if to ward off a chill.

"Why are you not in school today?" Dirk enunciates in his perfect Spanish. "Mi madre sent me here to wait for the touristas to take my photo," she responds (by way of Dirk's translation). I want to tell her that she shouldn't sit in the rain all day. I want to tell her just how precious she is, but instead, I smile and motion to her with my camera. As passersby in the lives of others, we are sometimes powerless to act outside the parameters of our brief encounters. We cannot impose our own values upon others. We cannot interfere or correct, according to our own mores. And so, it is with affection that I comply within the context of her request, and she is content with the money that she will bring home to her mother this day.

For some reason, I can't recollect much about where we went or what we did after this. Somewhere in my memory banks are fuzzy flashbacks of a conversation between a group of Austrian tourists remarking about a small white van that fell into the Urumbamba River ten days ago, killing all the passengers on board . . . gossip of banditos ambushing buses on the Pan American Highway . . . and more stories of stolen passports and slashed knapsacks. "Even the police will not help you!" Rather, I do recall clearly that at some point that afternoon, I held Dirk to a promise that he would read Isak Dinesen's short story, "The Dreaming Child," and I know for certain that I held myself to a promise to return to Ollantaytambo someday. Mostly, my mind was in a non-thinking mode, resting calmly in the quiet beauty surrounding me. No grinding. No reasoning. No thought. After all, said the Incas: "Silence is the Voice of the Great Spirit."

6
ART AND A DAY OF WANDERING

I never really had a chance to say a proper goodbye to Dirk. Last evening, while dining at the Chez Victor restaurant, Peter, an American student from Houston, Texas, persuaded Dirk and I to join him at a local after-club. It's not my style, but I reluctantly acquiesced, urged on by a growing coterie of well-intentioned travelers, only to find myself stranded at a disco, so aptly named "The Kamikaze."

A disco in Peru was just about the last place on earth I wanted to be. In fact, a disco, anywhere at anytime is about the last place I ever want to be. But it all began with Peter, and then the circle of disco-loving partygoers expanded in size and strength when he introduced us to his friends, Eric and Rita from San Francisco. Soon, there I was, catapulted galaxies away from "the world of the wondrous" and the local culture of Peru to the shock waves of metallic music, cigarette smoke, beer, and erstwhile hippies. As the decibel level of the raucous music left no possibility for any conversation at all, the five of us sat immobilized until 2am, rendered blind, deaf and speechless from the noxious clouds and noise.

By the time I made my excuses and returned to Los Marquesas Residential, I had missed curfew and found the great wooden gates guarding the entrance bolted shut. I tried calling out and pounding my fists on the door to no result, then set to scouring the streets searching for a nonexistent telephone. Adding to my dilemma was a sudden downpour of rain, causing my hair and clothes to get sopping wet. Cold, waterlogged, and without a room for the night, I made the snap decision to look for a dry spot under the colonnades at the Plaza De Armas. "I'll sit out with the homeless Cusqueños until morning," I resolved, observing of myself that I had no apprehension about doing this, whatsoever. Just in time to save me from myself, Dirk happened along out of nowhere, and horrified by my plans for the evening, urged me back to my hotel for another try at the doors. There we found two more curfew violators locked out and creating a fracas. Dirk and I joined in and the escalation of door bangers was rewarded when the innkeeper finally opened the gate, looking none too happy at our infringement of rule. Relief! Then, a mad dash inside to escape the rain—a rushed goodbye to Dirk, who was leaving for Amsterdam in the morning—and before I knew it the mighty double doors slammed shut behind me—such an inadequate farewell!

Yesterday morning, during the bus ride back to Cusco, Dirk was lulled into a sleepy haze by the rhythm of a bumpy ride along an unpaved road. Dozing on, and then off again, whenever the van hit a snag, he would easily vacillate between deep sleep and sudden awakening. Later, he recounted to me that in the course of this time he had had a dream that our bus was making a turn to cross a bridge, and as it did, the bus split in two—he going one way, and I, another. When an unusually sharp jolt on the road caused Dirk to awaken abruptly from his dream, he looked out the window to see the very same bridge he had envisioned while asleep—and just as had occurred in his dream, our van was making a turn to cross it. "Dirk's Dream" was perhaps as logical as it was prophetic, because this day would most likely be the day that I would purchase my ticket to La Paz and he would depart for the Netherlands.

> "How great art is! One is never really alone."
> —*Vincent Van Gogh*

I knew the value of art at an early age, not in terms of monetary value, but for the value of its companionship. And so it is, with street map in hand that I spend a good part of the morning of my last day in Cusco, walking the artist's sector of El Barrio de Los Artesanos. There I find many small galleries displaying the naïve art of the "Escuela Cuzqueña" (the Cusqueños School of Painting), which was originally founded by the Spaniards in the interest of promoting the conversion of the Incas to Christianity. With the ulterior motive of recruitment as a backset, Spanish artisans arrived in Peru to impart the techniques of drawing and oil painting that would nurture local talent while indoctrinating potential candidates on the merits of Catholicism. It is for this reason that Cusqueña paintings and sculpture are exclusively religious in nature.

The Cusqueña movement originally extended beyond the borders of Cusco-proper to the Spanish Creoles until the late seventeenth century when a wellspring of pride in Inca heritage prompted Cusco artisans to part ways and develop their own unique identity. Spearheaded by Diego Quispe Tito (1611-1681), a descendant of Inca nobles, and carried forward in the eighteenth century by the indigenous artist Marcos Zapanta (1710-1773), the Cusqueña style flourished in a mode that was less restrictive than the Spanish traditionalists. Characterized by one-dimensional flat images that were free from rule of schooled perspective technique, Cusqueña art depicted scenes of daily life in an explosion of bright red and yellow colors in stark contrast to the dark sober hues of their European counterparts.

I stroll the Barrio to browse the galleries and abundance of outdoor displays. With the simplicity of line and figure that is indicative of the naïve design of art, many of the paintings I see are complemented by the local flora and fauna specific to the region, with the mountainscape of a snow-capped Andes as a frequent backdrop. Paintings, both large and small, reflect the vicissitudes of ordinary peasant life; a llama carrying a load, a farmer picking beans in a field, a festival of the harvest. I am drawn to one painting in particular. It portrays a close and crowded Andean village where red-tiled roofs span the horizon from left to right of the canvas; the brilliant iron-red hue of the tiles are burnt flat against aquamarine hills that more closely resemble sand dunes in the shadows than the highest crests of the Andes. I consider how the innocence of folk art is so perfectly defined by the French term naïve, where the unfettered message of simplicity replaces the savoir-faire of prescribed technique.

The figurative sculptures that I come upon are crafted in a diversity of mediums. Some are molded in a paper maché mixture of wheat flour and plaster, then hand-painted in basic primary colors. Others are carved in unfinished woods and soapstone, or hand-etched and baked in a terra cotta earthenware. Many of the figures depict the saints of the Bible, the Virgin Mary, and the pervasive Christ figures that hang in agony from their crucifixes—all in a seamless fusion of Quechua and Western tradition.

I continue my walk past the Plaza of San Blas, then back down to the Churches of La Merced, and La Compagna de Jesus. At Calle Triunfo, a trio of American tourists gathers around the infamous polygonal block of twelve angles where two Quechua natives pose for photographs. Between the seams of a tapered alleyway, a red-tailed hawk soars past my view, revealing itself like a gift amid the grit and dust below it. Soon, I find myself back at the center of things at the main cathedral on the north side of the Plaza de Armas. I take a moment to revisit a unique eighteenth century painting by the mestizo artist Marcos Zapanta (also known as Marcos Sapaca Inca) that warrants a second look. Illustrative of the Cusqueños School of Painting, it depicts Jesus and the twelve apostles gathered around a table for the rites of the iconic Last Supper. But this is no ordinary portrayal of The Last Supper. There among the bread and fruit spread upon the table where Jesus and his disciples will dine together for the last time is a platter of *roast cuy*, otherwise known as roasted guinea pig. A Quechua delicacy (and very tasty, I'm told), the small rodent looks almost comical, lying on it's back with tiny feet pointed in the air—crisped to perfection. Examining the painting more closely, the chalice of the Eucharist is plainly seen, but the customary wine that will be transfigured into the blood of Christ has been displaced by chicha, the Inca beer distilled from corn maize. One more anomaly distinguishes this representation of The Last Supper—it is not without intention that the artist Zapanta has cleverly portrayed the face of Judas in the likeness of the invader Conquistador Francisco Pizarro. This painting is a prime example of the unique integration of Christianity and Quechua tradition that continues to endure in Peru. Through the juxtaposition of imagery, we may interpret irony, criticism, humor, and unwavering loyalty to ancestral heritage.

Perhaps befitting of this locale, it was here at the former site of Quiswarcancha, the great palace of Viracocha built for the Creator-God, that came the demise of the last Inca king with the mock trial and execution of Tupac Amaru, the third son of Manco Capac. Having grown increasingly intolerant to intermittent attacks on Spanish soldiers, and in an effort to eradicate the strong allegiance to the Sapa Inca that still prevailed among the natives, the new Viceroy Don Francisco de Toledo of Spain was to take a tougher approach to the conflict than did his predecessors. Under the pretense of a negotiation, Francisco dispatched a small envoy of the Spanish court into the dense jungle thicket. Their mission was to search for the Inca stronghold of Vilcabamba with the express purpose of luring Tupac Amaru back to Cusco. Unfortunately, the delegation had not make it very far when the plan backfired. Fiercely protective of their hidden sanctuary and understandably distrustful of any gesture of friendship since the unfortunate death of Tupac's brothers Titu Cusi and Sayri Tupac, advisors to the ruling Sapa Inca took pre-emptive action by ambushing the Spanish emissaries and killing them all. An enraged Don Francisco was provoked to dire consequence, from here on abandoning any arbitration of words for the force majeure of guns and swords. The Viceroy selected his very best for the task, consigning the imperturbable Captain Martin Garcia Oñez de Loyola, who had already gained fame by proving himself undefeatable in battle. With just a small battalion of armed troops, Garcia and his band of soldiers captured Tupac Amaru, bound him in chains, and officially declared him a prisoner of war. Then, the last Sapa Inca was returned to Cusco to meet his fate.

It was the year of 1572, when in a speedy mock trial Tupac Amaru was found guilty of atrocities against the state for the killing of the ambassadors of the court, even though he probably had nothing to do with it. Here, in the main square of the Plaza de Armas where I now sit, the last of the Sapa Incas was castigated with lances and whips until he would renounce his paganism and accept the precepts of Christianity in full view of the crowd that had gathered. Here, where I now set my gaze upon souvenir shops and colonnades, Tupac Amaru watched helplessly as his favorite wife was tied limb by limb to each of four horses, then ripped apart and dismembered. Over ten thousand spectators rounded the square as the Sapa Inca stepped up to the scaffold for his execution, and in a final gesture raised his hand to the wailing crowd. "Pachamama, witness how my enemies shed my blood!" he cried out to the earth goddess who embodied the birth of the first creation. And then, in the ultimate insult, Tupac Amaru was beheaded, not by a Spaniard, but by a Cañari Indian, whose tribe had allied themselves with the Spanish in their hatred of the Incas. In an instant, it was over. The head of Tupac Amaru was hitched to a pole and hoisted up in the plaza. The public display sent a message to one and all. Here perished the last of the Royal Incas.

Although the Conquistadores ended over three hundred years of Inca sovereignty with the capture and execution of Tupac Amaru, one feat would always elude them. They were never to find the mysterious city of Vilcabamba, the last refuge of the Inca. Where lies this asylum hidden deep within the cloud forest? Is Machu Picchu the lost city? Or is Vilcabamba still out there somewhere, waiting to be discovered? Archaeologists today are in general agreement that the Inca settlement of Espiritu Pampa, the relics of which are located in the dense jungle west of Cuzco, is most probably the true metropolis known as Vilcabamba. Ironically, Hiram Bingham had passed through Espiritu Pampa on his expedition, but did not believe this was the lost city of legendary note. I leave an open mind to any conclusion, but of this we can be sure—the most enduring legacy of the Kingdom of the Sun remains forever in the power of its secrets.

Business to do, I purchase my ticket to La Paz at the airline office on Avenida del Sol, exchange dollars at the local cambio, and check one last time at the station for the latest developments on the train to Machu Picchu. A street vendor paces the arcades, balancing a portable display of handcrafted jewelry in his open palms like a waiter offering a platter of hors d'oeuvres at a cocktail party. The silver is genuine and the handi-work is some of the best quality I've seen. I am assured of its genuine origin as well (from a local father/son team), and so I purchase a pair of thick silver earrings studded with large stones of amber and green turpentine that will be my pleasure to wear as both an adornment and a catalyzer of memory when I return home. In need of a new pair of walking shoes (since I only ever travel with one pair), I choose a set of pink sneakers, primarily for the red and blue llama pattern on the soles. In a bookstore, I am delighted to find Francisco Hidalgo's "Peru," a book of photographs I had been searching for. It is not without some deliberation that I decide to take on the burden of carrying it home through the rest of my journey.

"Hare Krishna!" Before I know it, I am halfway inside the door and too embarrassed to turn around and walk out. The restaurant I've entered offers Indian Health Food cuisine and is run by the well-meaning and overly eager members of a Hare Krishna sect, who zero in on their target and assail me with a barrage of good cheer and chants. A stickler for the ethnic experience of the country in which I am traveling, I am a bit taken aback to find myself in these surroundings as the object of so much attention. It is tantamount to the shock of the Kamikaze disco, last night. During times like these, I often think of the American author and humorist Mark Twain and wonder with what sarcasm he would have notated this scenario in his travel journals. Perhaps, he need not have added much other than his astute observations of the details as they present themselves, seeing how the incongruity of this circumstance clearly speaks for itself.

Back to my room, I light a rose tea candle and spread my map of South America across the bedspread. With an orange highlighter pen, I trace the course of my journey ahead in zigzag lines across the page. It is not exactly the shortest path between two points that is the anticipated route before me, and it is certainly not the most practical. By air, I'll fly to Cusco-to-Lima-to-La Paz, Bolivia, and then take a bus to Copacabana and Lake Titicaca for a visit. When I'm ready to return to Peru, I'll travel overland back across the border with a stop in Puno, followed by a train to Cusco—and hopefully, if my timing is right, onwards to Machu Picchu when the strike is over.

About a year ago, I had a dream. Not just an ordinary dream, but one of those lucid dreams of a rare quality where the vivid intensity of the experience is as real as a waking one. In the dream, I saw myself standing below a green rise of lush tropical mountains. There was a dirt road and a brown river below. I could feel the atmosphere around me, close with a light mist of rain. I was saying goodbye to someone and I recall that the goodbye was poignant. Something about the parting consoled me, but I didn't know why. In this dream, I felt a distinct air of anticipation of what lie ahead. There was no sense of heaviness or worry. I was happy and free from burden—light, exhilarated, and filled with vitality. I was on my way to something spectacular. But whom was I saying goodbye to? And where was I going?

Outside, the night air holds still. The calm of the evening is only disturbed by the rallying cries of Runa demonstrators picketing in the town square. It is almost 2AM when I blow out the rose tea candle, snuggle under the layers of blankets warming my bed and close my eyes to the pitch black of my room.

7
DETOURS

"Why go to the moon when you can go to La Paz?" say the locals when speaking about their unusual city, which at 13,000 feet in the Andean mountain range sits in a bowl-like crater rivaling the most barren moonscape. That this is an impoverished country and of the most dire conditions in South America is as apparent to the eye as is the sharpened snow-capped peaks of the Cordillera Real that rims the city edges. Although mining is the leading industry of Bolivia, with twelve percent of the worlds tin originating from here, much of the country remains economically underdeveloped. Almost half the population of Bolivia earns their living by farming, but a mere two percent of the land has been cultivated, and presently only four hundred miles of road have been paved in the entire country.

There is a quiet here. People speak softly and move slowly. The quiet parallels the visual of the somber landscape. Much of what I see is brown and dry, barren and sparse; a stark transition from the lush vegetation of the Peruvian Sacred Valley.

"Where is she going?" I ask of no one in particular, as I roll down the car window and stretch my neck out to follow the footpath of an elderly woman ascending one of the sheer cliffs, just outside the city limits. Above her, a crude hole that serves as a window is hacked into the layered sediment of rock, revealing the startling presence of a cliff dwelling. This Aymara Indian, who makes her home in a cave, is one of the last remaining descendants of the builders of Tiahuanaco, an ancient pre-Colombian city, whose ruins lie in the high deserts of Western Bolivia. Distinguished from the Quechua by their derby hats and muted colors, the Aymara population of La Paz now represents more than one-half of its over one million residents.

When my taxi arrives at my destination of Illampu Street in the Indian Quarter, I hesitate to get out of the car. It looks as if there's been an earthquake here. Chunks of broken limestone lay askew on the sidewalk alongside the crumbling walls of decrepit buildings overrun with graffiti. Homeless vagrants nap in the ameliorating heat of day, while directly above their heads shards of broken glass dangle precariously from the strategically placed trundles of barbed wire that crown the defended rooftops. For a moment, I am a bit put off to the tough streets of poverty, but I make the choice to stay here in the Indian Quarter, rather than in the modern sector of the city on the other side of La Paz.

Inside the doors of my hotel, I am welcomed with kindness. I'm given a double room for the price of a single and surprisingly, it has all the necessities—a working telephone, a heater, warm blankets, a private bath, and even a nice writing table and chair. So far, I can breathe adequately in the higher altitude, but I already have hints of a headache. At 13,000 feet, I have ascended almost two thousand feet higher in elevation than Cusco. When I open the plastic film cans to load my camera, the lids pop open like champagne corks from the sheer pressure of the rarified air. At this altitude it is difficult to keep a match lit and it's no wonder that there isn't a need for a fire department here.

On this rather chilly first day in La Paz, I am soon out the door and making my way downhill to Calle Sagarnaga—what is surely one of the most unusual streets in the world. Here, the Witches Market (Mercado de Hechiceria or Mercado de las Brujas) with its magic charms, medicinal herbs and paraphernalia, begins at San Francisco Church and extends over one mile up into the winding hills. A dried llama fetus buried under your house will bring you good fortune; a skull and crossbones will deter the Angel of Death; special incense burned at the appointed time will keep your cows healthy; and talismans placed over your bed will bring you long life. Although most Aymara are devout Catholics, very much akin to the Quechua, ancient symbols and superstitions remain important to religious observance and faith.

The avenue of Calle Sagarnaga is a feast for the eyes and I barely know where to look first. Bales of colored pebbles—red, yellow and green, curiously carved alabaster charms, owl feathers, and the desiccated skins of the highly prized guinea pig all compete for my view. With a come hither waving of her hands, one Aymara witch distinguishes herself from the rest when she motions for me to squat down beside her on the ground. Tipping the rim of her derby hat to block out the glare of the morning sun, the old Aymara grabs a scrap of newspaper, crumples it in the palm of her hand and begins to prepare a potpourri of magic. There are no words spoken between us as she sprinkles a handful of dried earth, some tiny speckles of silver, a spattering of red and yellow beans, then exactly six green stones and two alabaster hands into a mix. I watch her as she twists a tuft of multi-colored wool into a string, and then spreads it in a circle over the top. Still busily unfolding her mysteries to me, the old woman reaches deep into a burlap sack and retrieves a golden charm of a man and woman, arm in arm. When she offers it to me, I break my silence: "Que es esto?" I ask.

"Para matrimonio (*for marriage*)," she replies.

A pink alabaster fetish, engraved with the image of a house, follows next. "Para su casa (*for your home*)," she instructs, holding it up to my face for inspection. From its rectangular shape, I recognize this to be a *mysteriosos*, a small amulet that is typically two inches in length and whose flat surface accommodates a variety of motifs that may be inscribed. Its purpose is comparable to that of the Christian *ex votos*, a votive or offering to a saint or divinity.

For a second, my mind slips out of the present and in to the mindful awareness that I am a traveler having a cherished experience of the most unusual kind; permitted to enter unto to the clandestine world of an Aymara witch.

"Para salud (*for health*)," she continues, revealing to me another small talisman carved with a cross and two circles—and then, a ceramic figure of a man and woman with arms and legs entwined, representing what I would guess to be, fertility. "Muy importante," she says.

I remain silent, kneeling on the ground beside her, my eyes scanning the activity around me and taking it all in. Standing in a doorway, a young female, perhaps the daughter of an Aymara witch, finds shelter from the searing heat near the colorful paraphernalia of her mother's wares. She is the embodiment of the next generation of females who will inherit the traditions of her ancestors to one day take her mother's place as an Aymara sorcerer. What treasures of hidden knowledge are passed down through generations in these rituals of wizardry and superstition, I wonder? And what untold mysteries lay behind the sun-weathered lines of these beautiful faces?

As I stand up to leave, the Aymara witch guides me back down by the arm. She reaches under a red cloth bushel and emerges with three stone sculptures cradled in her hands. "Pachamama, Pachamama," she mumbles, repeatedly. I recognize the name *Pachamama* as that of the ubiquitous Aymaran Earth Mother who presides over the critical harvest. Notably, the legacy of this Earth Mother's male counterpart, her deity-husband Pachacamac *(Pacha Kamaq)*, the Earth Maker and creator god who pre-dated the Incas, has all but evaporated in the face of his Inca rival, Viracocha. That the mythology of Pachamama was permitted to endure may signify a gesture of abatement to the gods of harvest on the part of the Incas, who often placated their adversaries, rather than provoke them. Indeed, with a fierce dragoness power to her motherly instincts, Pachamama brings good fortune, fertility and protection; but also holds the vengeful wrath of earthquake in her rounded arsenal.

Similar in likeness to the clean lines of primitive North American Eskimo art, each of the stoneworks placed in my hands are chiseled with multiple faces that can see in all directions, suggesting a level of vigilance to the deity. Two of the sculptures have serpents wrapped around the neck of the main figurehead, and all have embracing arms. One can only conjecture that the presence of the snake, commonly regarded in mythological lore as a symbol of fertility, represents the generative virtue of the life-giving force that sheds and renews itself, while its poisonous sting defends the ground of which it is guardian. I try not to react as I examine the curious stone carvings. She hands me two more.

. . .

It rained huge hailstones in the night. I have it on good word that it is indeed Summer here, despite the marble-sized balls of ice rapping on the windowpanes this morning. Yesterday afternoon, I lay down for a one-hour nap and didn't wake up until this morning, still dressed in my street clothes and sweating from the blast of the space heater. I probably overdid it yesterday, walking almost eight miles on my first day in this high elevation.

Finding a clean place for an American breakfast is my first goal this morning as I head down towards Avenue de 16 Julio in the modern sector of La Paz. Otherwise known as the Prado, this main street and center of activity runs from the statue of Bolivar (the city's namesake) in Plaza Venezuela to the statue of Sucre in the Plaza Tamayo. As contrasted with the narrow winding hills of the Indian Quarter, the business-oriented side of La Paz is characterized by its wide avenues of people and cars. Somewhat fragmented and in a state of disrepair, even this part of the city looks defeated to me. Its graying landscape is a mélange of glass and steel apartment buildings, offices, and hotels, all blandly constructed in box-shaped architectural monotony. Curiously, the generators that provide electricity for these buildings are driven by waterfalls of melting snow from the surrounding mountain range of the Altiplano. It's no wonder that blackouts are not uncommon. The *Altiplano*, Spanish for "high plain" or "high plateau" designates that area of the Andes at its broadest spread, and which by character produces a natural drainage basin for water.

I find a breakfast of scrambled eggs, toast, orange juice and coffee at one of the pricier hotel restaurants. The meal is satisfactory, but I realize afterwards that the waiter has cheated me on the bill. After exchanging one hundred American dollars for millions of Bolivian pesos, I spend most of the day searching for a city bus or tour to Tiahuanaco, the pre-Colombian ruin site thirty-eight miles outside of La Paz. "Not enough tourists in La Paz," I'm told, by one travel agent after another. Apparently, it takes at least six people to warrant the rental of a mini-van, and so far, I am the only visitor interested in going to Tiahuanaco this week. I'm offered a private car and driver, but the cost is excessive. "Not enough people," is the echo of response to my query, over and again.

On the south side of town, a traffic jam is causing a huge commotion. Apparently, a consortium of students and miners has mobilized to block the main roads. They are in protest of the ten coalmines that were recently shut down by the government, resulting in many jobs lost. The military is on the streets in full-force, armed with sub-machine guns and riot gear. They are preparing to tear-gas the protestors. I don't even dare to take a photo, after the story I recently heard about a tourist being pulled off an airplane for attempting to shoot a photograph of security forces at the airport. He was interrogated for hours, with his film and camera confiscated before he was released. I stuff my Nikon tight into my shoulder bag and begin walking briskly. Once past the main business street of Calle Mercado, the government palace, and the Cathedral at Plaza Murillo, I scrap my map and points-of-interest guide and speed up to a quickened pace in order to escape the commotion behind me. I have no idea where I'm going, but once far from the shouts of protestors, I follow my instincts, inspecting the nooks and crannies of corners and alleyways, and guiding myself by whatever sights draw me towards them. Traces of American culture lie in such fine detail; the sound of rock n' roll wafts out a storefront window where bootleg CD's are sold; and at the local cinema, a duplicity of posters depicting the image of a ferocious King Kong (looking much more tempestuous than I remember him) are prominently displayed. "Yankee, Sale de Sud!" *(Yankee, leave South America!)* demands the intimidating graffiti, dripping in blood-red paint across the entire width of a twenty-foot wall—all this, smack in the face of the Superman dolls and Batman masks that are for sale on this very same street. "They love us and they hate us," I think, while reminding myself that I am a citizen of the world, and not solely an American.

It's no surprise when my meandering trail leads me back to the Indian Quarter at the site of the Central Market on Avenida Camacho. I browse through piles of rugs and blankets, but for some reason, none of the vendors will bargain with me. I have better luck purchasing an *Ekkekko*, a painted plaster doll that represents the God of Abundance. The "Ekkekko" (meaning midget or dwarf) is about seven inches in height and is fashioned in the likeness of what may at first sight look to be a street vendor selling his wares. But this is no run-of-the-mill man of commerce; this is the crafted projection of the "Deity of Bounty," Bolivian-style.

Draped in a colorfully striped poncho woven of the precious aguayo fabric that is hand-loomed from the wool of the alpaca, he is capped with a traditional *chullo*, the knit headpiece customary to the Andeans. The Ekkekko carries on its back, arms and chest all the essentials that are required for a full and fruitful life in the coming year. A satchel of rice, a clay pot for cooking, bags of sugar, herbs, grain, a pair of sandals, a dollar bill, and a tiny house and truck are among the miniature trinkets pinned to his outstretched arms and body.

Each January, the three-week observance of "Alasitas," *The Festival of Abundance*, is celebrated at the Parque Urbano in La Paz, offering a variety of miniature charms and mysteriosos (the rectangular talismans carved with images) to match the complete plethora of personal wishes that may be conjured. In this annual ritual, Bolivians traditionally pin the miniature curios onto the Ekkekko doll and place it in their homes as an altarpiece where they may direct with prayer their desires to be granted. Under the rim of his handlebar moustache, the Ekkekko's mouth is open in a gesture that suggests he is ready to receive his offering. Often mistaken for the intimation of a yell, his open mouth is poised to receive the gift of a cigarette from his petitioners. A throwback to the Aymaran god Ekkekko, the benefactor of good harvest, in some parts of Bolivia the festival of Alasitas is synchronized to take place in the spring, coincident to the advent of cropping.

At Illampu Vegetable Market, I can no longer restrain myself from attempting a photograph of the exotic Aymara natives, so beguiling in their colorful garments. Coarser in appearance and of a demeanor more sullen and poker-faced than the Quechua, the women are garbed in their derby hats, billowing shawls, and multi-layered skirts called "polleras" whose heavy folds of fabric protect from the cold. Not to be outdone, the men in their striped ponchos and knitted caps called "chullos" are quite a vision for the foreign eye to behold. I pause at a fruit stand, stacked with beet-red mangoes where a makeshift awning provides the four women under it some shade from the scorching rays of the afternoon sun. I ask permission to snap a photo, but all of four of them decline my request, even when I offer payment. Moving onwards through the marketplace, I notice that many of the locals turn their backs as they spot my camera, in an attempt to foil any potential request. I make one last effort to shoot from a distance. Fumbling under the hindrance of a manual zoom lens, I rush to make adjustments while the sun goes in and out, but the market women are wise to this and begin to throw pits at me. Some look angry, but others look frightened. I become acutely aware that I may be imposing upon persons who are fearful of the mere sight of a camera. Superstition holds among the natives that it is bad luck for one's spirit to be captured on a photograph. When I realize this, I stop immediately.

In what seem mere moments, the sky grows dark and it begins to pour buckets of rain without warning. Ducking under the canopy of a hotel entrance, I crouch down on the cool concrete steps to wait for the torrent to let up. The desk clerk, whose nametag reads "Ivar", emerges to join me with the intention of practicing his English on me while I am held captive. When I confide to him my problem of finding a way to Tiahuanaco, he suggests that I inquire once again at my own hotel. "Several Peace Corps workers have arrived in town, today," he informs me.

The nearby Chinese Restaurant has been closed since I arrived here, as has the highly recommended Bolivian restaurant serving local dishes such as chuños and picantes. Finding a hygienic place to eat dinner on this side of town has not been easy. Most of the family run kitchens don't exactly meet American standards of an "A" rating, but the neat lace curtains of one rain-spattered window persuade me to stop in one of them.

Inside the private home turned-restaurant, Hector and Maria, the proprietor and his wife, greet me warmly. They switch on the lights, which might otherwise be turned off for economical purposes, and ask me what I'd like to eat. Most of the items I suggest, they don't have, so I settle for what I can get—which is namely, eggs. I'm hungry and very grateful for the hospitality, so I stay. Maria gets to business, wiping off the table, while Hector fires up the stove. A small boy, whom I assume to be a son or relative, brings a scrap of paper and hands me a pencil. He inquires in a spartan English what I'd like for breakfast tomorrow morning and signals for me to write it down. "Everything fine," he says. "Now is good." There are many smiles to fill the gap of words that are unable to be articulated, and in instances like these, I remind myself that language is only ten percent of communication. Surely, I have discovered in my travels that such is the case time and time again that the individual who attempts to express themselves in a so-called "broken" language may so often "break my heart" by choosing the wrong word that is at last, the more correct word. A bit off terminology, but oh so much more to the core of understanding, the impact of the chosen word from individual to foreigner (and perhaps, vice versa) has the capacity to instantaneously dissolve boundaries by way of an emotional contact. Once, when crossing by ferry over the Bosphorus in Istanbul, I befriended a woman and her son for the brief interval of a boat ride. I could not speak but a few words of Turkish and she could not speak but a few words of English, yet we made a connection through gesture and fits of giggles at the ineptness of our attempts. As we approached the harbor where she would disembark, the woman stood and rapped her closed hand over her chest three times, in the way that Turkish people do when they simulate the beating of a heart. She spoke in a slow staccato-like beat when she said: "We are same heart." Even now, thinking back, I am touched by these words.

In such a way, Hector, Maria and the little boy are not merely nondescript restaurateurs who will feed me dinner tonight, but are transcended by their humanity as a mother, father and son— sympatico in the collective condition of joy and struggle, irrespective of language or culture. Hopefully, my status as a tourist-at-large is likewise overridden.

When I check in at the service desk of my hotel, I discover that I am already booked on a mini-van to Tiahuanaco tomorrow. Four more travelers are on the trip with me. I wonder who they are.

8

STONE IN THE CENTER

"Well, which is it? Do you live in New York, or do you live in Los Angeles?" she demanded to know, folding her arms with a definitive pounce and staring straight into my eyes, as if directing a laser beam of light right through me. This being my introduction to Toni, a Peace Corps worker stationed in Paraguay, who is one of the passengers on my mini-van to Tiahuanaco this morning. Her cohort and fellow Peace Corps worker, Sandy, lowers her eyes and blushes an embarrassed smile, offering no comment. The two Australians look straight ahead, in silence.

"I was born and raised in New York, and I live in Los Angeles," I explain, while wondering why I have to spell this out under duress of an interrogation.

Toni flashes me an odd look, measuring somewhere between suspicion and disgust. The popular phrase "she-is-a-piece-of-work" comes to mind. Born and raised in the historic coal-mining town of Hazelton, Pennsylvania, Toni's true name is Catherine, but she prefers to be called Toni, for short. Perhaps, this discrepancy of moniker accounts for the reason she is so sensitive to the alternate choice of city names that have been my residence. Educated in the most orthodox of parochial schools and then married by the age of twenty-one in the tradition customary to her generation, Toni gave it all up at the age of fifty-four to join the Peace Corps. With her children grown and out of the house, one day she just announced to her steelworker hubby that she was moving out and on to follow her life-long dream, and since then, she has never looked back.

That Toni is a woman clear in her ways is reflected by the fact that she makes not even the slightest attempt at a Spanish accent when speaking the Spanish language. She, and her traveling companion Sandy, a grade-school teacher from Ohio, are serving their volunteer time in a small jungle village east of Concepción, where they teach the basics of hygiene and nutrition to the Guarani Indians. I am all ears on the two-hour ride to Tiahuanaco. As our battered grey van engages in a hapless race against the broad base of Mt. Illimani, I am both entertained and informed to hear about the day an army of red ants invaded Sandy's hut; the superstitions of the village women, who believe they will die if they take a hot bath after drinking milk; and the relentless rains of the monsoon season with their devastating floods. "Could I give it all up to join the Peace Corps?" I ask myself.

The archaeological site of Tiahuanaco, once the imperial center of the Aymara civilization, stretches across a desolate platform, seemingly devoid of life from all directions for as far as the eye can see. Here, tall stone monoliths, weeping gods, and walls of faces with their quizzical expressions stand amongst geometrically precise aqueducts and temples, posing unanswered questions for archaeologists today. Scientists speculate that this city of over 50,000 people once sat upon the shores of Lake Titicaca, only thirteen miles away, but that the waters receded over time. Native legend has it that the city of Tiahuanaco was constructed in a single night, that its inhabitants disappeared into the jungles of Amazonia, and that a hidden subterranean tunnel system links it to the sacred city of Cusco in Peru. Indeed, traces of Tiahuanaco art have been found as far away as Ecuador to the north and Chile and Argentina to the south. Little is known of its lost inhabitants, sophisticated peoples who devised their own calendar, hieroglyphics, and advanced socio-political system. The city is believed to have been occupied as recently as 2,000 years ago and most scientists agree that Tiahuanaco achieved its greatest peak of affluence around 600 AD. By 900 AD, it had been inexplicably abandoned.

As we approach the center of the ruin site, we face the Kalassaya (Standing Stones) Temple, which is speculated to have once been a great ceremonial compound. Standing alone in a large sunken courtyard beneath the main plaza are three stone monoliths of peculiar expression. They are enclosed by a rectangular wall measuring 442 by 426 feet, embedded with rows of faces. In likeness to the fortifications found in Peru, the stones are carved and fit together with the utmost of skill and without the support of any mortar, whatsoever.

A few yards from the main structure, a figure hewn of granite gazes past the barren plains; his vacant eyes staring into nowhere. That he is a celestial being or demi-god of some importance is evidenced by the scepter he holds in his hands, a symbol often seen on carvings, textiles, and pottery from the Tiahuanaco era denoting a leader or commander of the people. It is noteworthy that Tiahuanaco culture exerted a profound influence on the Incas, who discovered this sacred site about 1200 AD and then adapted some of the symbology for their own. The religious symbols of the sun, the puma, and the condor (revered for its ability to reach heights that no human being could attain) appear frequently in both Aymara and Inca art.

The most distinguished of the archaeological finds at Tiahuanaco is the much heralded Gateway to the Sun, an archway chiseled from a solid chunk of andesite weighing almost twelve tons. At the apex of the gateway is a large relief figure thought to represent the creator-deity Viracocha, also known here as the Weeping God for the teardrops depicted falling from his eyes. Substantiating his stature as a royal is an elaborate headdress suggesting the rays of the sun, the two ruling scepters he holds in his hands, and the forty-eight half-man/half-bird relief figures that are probably his attendants. A large crack from an earthquake has scarred a split into the stone, a minor defect considering the centuries of exposure. I wonder out loud if the teardrops falling from his eyes might more accurately represent the gold sweat of the sun, but no one can answer this.

Feeling restless, I move away from the group to go exploring on my own. Kneeling to sift through the dry parched sand, I find broken chips of brown pottery and a few turquoise-blue stones that I leave in place, respecting the integrity of the ruin site. I spot a raised area of hard cracked earth and begin to amuse myself by experimenting with my macro-lens, shooting textured close-up shots while getting acquainted with the oversensitive red dot on my light meter—when suddenly there comes a voice from behind me: "Is that your camera or isn't it?" snarls Toni.

At the pizzeria on Avenue Manco Capac, the waiter brings us a platter of thick crust pizza smothered with chopped tomatoes, black olives, and cheese; something I have not set eyes on since leaving home. The dinner permits me the time to get acquainted with Bill and Sharon, a pair of travelers from Australia, who have roughed their way across Bolivia suited with sleeping bags and professional camping gear. They are aiming for the sight of Halley's Comet at Machu Picchu as the climax of their trip. I probe them about their travels to the cities of Potosi, Sucre and the jungles of Chulumani, but they are besotted by the romanticism of San Francisco and its hippie culture, preferring to talk about that instead. Their California dream is to ride a motorcycle from the Golden Gate Bridge from San Francisco along the coast of Big Sur continuing all the way down Highway One to Santa Barbara. I have made this magnificent journey dozens of times (albeit, not by motorcycle) and I heartily encourage their game plan, providing them with suggestions for scenic stops, along the route.

"If the witches on Calle Sargarnaga wouldn't speak to me, why would they speak to you?" barks Toni, as our travel-chat turns to the subject of the Witchcraft Market. "I went back there three times and not a word. They totally ignored me. Now, why would they speak to you?" she recants.

It becomes obvious to me that for whatever reasons are whirling through her psyche, a theme of skepticism is threaded throughout Toni's dialogue.

"Let's try again tomorrow," chokes Sandy, who enters into an uncontrollable coughing fit that ends our conversation. Toni runs to get her some mineral water. It was only just yesterday that our hotel manager had an oxygen tank brought to Sandy's room when she became breathless following a short hike up the steep hills of the Indian Quarter. Toni is concerned that Sandy's high blood pressure condition may be exacerbated by the rarified air, which can cause heart attack or stroke, and rightly insists that she visit a doctor tomorrow morning.

The waiter brings us a hot kettle of maté de coca to calm our nerves and stomachs. Conversation at the table moves towards a discussions of whether or not to stay in La Paz for the rest of the week or move on. For me, the seeds of departure have been planted. I am feeling a bit oppressed by the bleakness of the city and its been taking a concentrated effort of clear thought to keep my spirits steady here. Even the lure of safety in companionship won't change my plans. I'm ready to break away from the confines of what has evolved to be a traveling cartel and have already quietly decided to leave this rooftop of the world for lower ground. I'll move on to Copacabana at the shores of Lake Titicaca and then to Puno, where I'll edge my way back to the Sacred Valley in Peru, when the train strike is over. Bill and Sharon make attempts to convince me to stay, but I decline. I may or may not meet up with them in Copacabana if our schedules overlap.

. . .

At the time of day called dusk, that crack in time between daylight and evening that the Scottish so aptly call the gloaming, the soft blue glow of twilight carried the skies for a few brief minutes of grandeur as we rode into the Valley de Las Lunas, otherwise known as the *Valley of the Moon*. With just a brief taxi ride from La Paz, we are met with a panoramic vista of iron-red mountains where in the foreground a huge gorged canyon of icicle-like rock formations create a strange and eerie landscape, very reminiscent to me of Bryce Canyon in Utah. A number of maze-like footpaths lead down into the steep gorge below. I follow one of them, interjecting myself alongside a dominion of stone, where dozens of enormous cone-shaped peaks, together forged by wind, time, and the unknown, hold autonomy. As the sun begins to sink below the range of iron, I hike alongside a ridge of pointed towers to get a better view of the impending sunset. Orange rays glitter across the white rock columns whose granite stipple sparkles with diamonds of reflected light. I linger to take a deep breath. It comes as a feeling of respite. To know the triumph of the sunset seems a divine intervention from the somber streets of La Paz.

9

THE WOMB OF MANKIND

Before, the world was dark and on all the earth there was no life, until at once, the Supreme God Viracocha rose from shimmering waters of Lake Titicaca, and with his bare hands created the glories of the Sun, the Moon and the Stars. From the clay of the large island at the center of the lake, he cast the image of Manco Capac, the first Sun God and ruler to whom all other Gods on earth would from this moment onwards, be servile. And from the smaller island of the lake, he fashioned a companion and sister/wife for the Sapa-Inca, whose name was Mama Ocllo. It was then that whole nations sprang from the formlessness of the primordial waters along with the caves, the trees, the hills, and all that was now holy. With the first breath of life on the first day of light, the great God Viracocha ordered the peoples of the world to gather forth and follow him in all directions, travelling underground beneath the great flood to find their way. Wherever the Sun God rested his staff upon emergence from the underground maze would be deemed the center of a sacred empire—and that center was Cusco.

It's an uncanny parallel to the Book of Genesis that would stand as a textbook example of the collective consciousness for any Jungian proponent. Indeed, numerous archetypal patterns may be found in the Inca creation myth. Viracocha's first invocations are the celestial planets that provide Light; the sun, the moon and the stars. A compatible motif is found in the Old Testament of the Hebrew Bible whereby the first act of creation is the invocation of Light "Let there be Light" (Genesis 1:14) out of the depths of darkness that pervade the earth. The emergence of light that follows the primordial void is seen universally in religions from the Koran to the Vedas, to Taoism and Buddhism.

That the Creator-God Viracocha fashions the first man and woman from materials of the earth described as clay or stone is a symbolic act that embodies the manifestation of spirit into flesh. Both clay and stone are symbols of shapeless matter that hold the promise of "becoming" for many nature-based cultures. The first man, Manco Capac, is created from materials of the larger island of the Sun, corresponding to the symbol of the male; while the first woman, Mama Occlo is created from the smaller island of the Moon, representing the symbol of the feminine. This distinction in status between the two beings provides insight into the spiritual values of the society. The dynamics of a larger and a smaller island tells us that the male Sun God is more powerful than the female Moon-Goddess. Apparently, patriarchy exists at the time the creation myth is written or transmuted orally. The story also provides the population with a vision of universal balance between the masculine/feminine and active/receptive elements of nature in the cosmos.

The reference to a flood that engulfs the land is also a common theme in ancient mythologies. It is an indication that either the newly created beings of Inca myth are born in sin and must be purified—or almost immediately have broken moral code and become separated from divine purpose, catalyzing a great deluge to wash away their transgressions. In much the same way does the famous mythological ark of Noah sail the waters of a great flood carrying everything on board that is needed for the restoration of species once the torrential overflow has receded. In the destruction sent by the flood, a death/rebirth cycle is implied. Indeed, Viracocha decrees his creations to a trial by fire, instructing them to enter down in to the caves and tunnels of the underground until the floodwaters recede. The dark, moist and trough like emptiness of the caves may be representative of the maternal womb, a place of rebirth and initiation whereby the people will be born again. The labyrinth of the hollowed tunnels point the way that Viracocha's creations must search for goodness and truth in order to emerge to a new consciousness.

This Inca creation myth ends with a prognostication that the point at which the Sapa Inka surfaces and sets his stake to the ground will be declared the navel of the universe. A new beginning, and with it, a new history for the making is implied. The navel, or *omphalos*, is an archetypal symbol of the center of the world and is the reason why Lake Titicaca, that body of water elevated to the metaphorical edge of the heavens, is regarded by the Andeans as the womb of mankind with Cusco as its navel. It's also the reason why the residents who inhabit these shores consider themselves to be the oldest peoples in the world.

The four-hour bus ride from La Paz to Copacabana is a passage over a relentlessly crude, uneven road, which intermittently routes through the notorious Pan American Highway. I can now guess the reason why it is that the majority of persons pay the additional dollars to take the hydrofoil or overnight steamer, instead.

Lake Titicaca is so enormous that at times its expanse appears as an ocean to my eye. Over one hundred and forty miles long and seventy miles across at its widest point, it covers an area over three thousand square miles. The lake is so large that from my vantage point on the bus, its boundaries cannot be seen at once, giving me the illusion that I'm looking at the sea lapping upon its shore, rather than a lake swaddling its banks. Poised 12,500 feet on the Altiplano between Bolivia and Peru, Lake Titicaca holds the title of the highest navigable lake in the world.

When I finally arrive at the main plaza of Copacabana, the atmosphere is still. My guidebook leads me to believe that this is a gay and festive city, a virtual carnival of cheer; the "original Copacabana" party-town, where townspeople run to greet the bus to welcome visitors—but today, it is a ghost town. Situated on the edge of the lake between Mount Calvario and Mount Nino Calvario, Copacabana is home to over six thousand residents, but I wonder where they are? Since it's too early for siesta, I begin to think that I'm here at the wrong time of year, or that perhaps some widespread evacuation has occurred that I'm not aware of. Other than two shirt-sleeved men standing motionless on a street corner, there is not a soul to be seen.

As the port comes into view, I don't sight any of the infamous balsa reed boats built by the Suriqui Indians, nor do I see one of the fantastical foot-long frogs I've heard so much about. The snow-capped peaks that followed my bus have disappeared from view, and only the lake that feigns to be a sea transcends expectation.

In May of 1969, the Norwegian ethnographer and adventurer Thor Heyerdahl set out to cross the Atlantic from Africa to the Americas in a papyrus reed boat named "Ra," so named in honor of the Egyptian Sun God. Having taken note of the similarity between Egyptian reed boats crafted of papyrus as portrayed in ancient Egyptian art to the vessels of South America constructed of the buoyant balsa reed, Heyerdahl became passionate to prove that the Egyptians could have negotiated the Atlantic on such a vessel. Unfortunately, 2,600 miles out to sea, the Ra Expedition was aborted when the ship that Heyerdahl had built so carefully to specification, suffered irreparable damage in a fierce storm. Ever determined to prove his theory, an unyielding Heyerdahl arrived in Bolivia for a second attempt, but this time he would solicit the help of the Aymara Indians, whose boat-building skills most closely resemble those of the ancient Egyptians. In the year 1970, the ship named "Ra 2" successfully completed the 3,270-mile voyage from Morocco to Barbados in just fifty-seven days. It is with great interest that I come to explore the origins of Ra 2, which I had the good fortune of seeing in person on a prior trip to Norway.

Back at the main plaza, there is at last a little action. Perhaps the town is just waking up. A few street vendors lay out their wares on white plastic café tables with blue striped umbrellas, under which I assume they will take shelter from the high-elevation sunlight. As I am obviously a tourist, I should be primary material for a sale, but there is no active sense of commerce aimed at me at all—no shouting, no calling, no come hither gestures. I stroll by the tables to browse the goods and notice that each of the counters display the redundancy of identical holy medals and rosary beads—and oh yes, a few balsa reed boats on key chains, but I refuse to buy a keychain with a balsa reed boat, when I haven't seen one yet.

A band of school children, attired in maroon-colored uniforms, skip past me singing aloud. But once out of sight, it is again strangely quiet and subdued. If this were the month of August, this plaza would be alive with activity for the annual "Blessing of the Engines." In a one-of-a-kind ceremony that must be a fascinating sight to behold, dozens of buses and trucks, draped with colorful blossoms, line up in front of the church waiting to be blessed by the presiding priest in an effort to gain absolution from mechanical problems for the ensuing year. In view of the fact that the low oxygen content of the high altitude air directly affects the air/fuel combustion of an engine, this unusual ritual is of critical necessity. Other annual celebrations, such as Independence Day, Christmas, the Easter Candlelight Procession and Spring Fiesta are all occasions that have probably given Copacabana its reputation for a carnival-like atmosphere. It's just not my week for a carnival, I guess.

The magnificent Basilica of Our Lady of Copacabana that graces the central plaza is a dazzling sight to behold—quite literally. Its playful architectural style is a medley of sixteenth century Spanish Colonial, Moorish and Contemporary influences. Completely restored from the pillage of the Latin American Wars of Independence in the late eighteenth and early nineteenth centuries with a fresh coat of white paint, the sight of the basilica is almost blinding against the glare of the afternoon sun. With its multiple domes, atrium, and striking mosaic trim of terra cotta and steel green color, this large and rambling construction is an engineering feat to outdo all others in its class; its only rival for attention, the grand Lake of Titicaca itself. It is with a flash of showmanship that the huge compound housing the shrine of the Virgin of Copacabana stretches across one entire end of the plaza in order to accommodate four smaller chapels; each of them containing three golden crosses six feet tall or more. I explore the edges of the chapel exterior with my camera, capturing angles of abstract shapes against the opaque blue sky. Inside, the main church is a treasure lode of seventeenth century paintings, along with the highly prized sixteenth century rendering of the Dark Virgin of the Lake, believed by Andeans to have miracle-working powers.

At the Hotel Playa Azul, accommodations are full board with three meals a day. In a display of impressive organization, I am seated for dinner at a table marked "Table #43," a match for my room number. The dining is a bit formal, but the waiter seems proud and dignified. It is a lovely meal of sopa con pan (soup with bread), chuño (a local potato dish), fresh fried fish (from the lake, perhaps?) and a crepe for dessert. Over the cantina, leans an old television set whereon an adult male is jabbering speedily in Spanish, utilizing a chalk and blackboard to instruct on the logic of algebraic formulas. I notice that the scanty mix of locals seated with me in the dining room are absolutely fixated on the television screen, literally hypnotized by the sight of the gentleman teaching algebra. This is either a case of the insidious manner by which the television screen dominates our attention to the exclusion of our surroundings—or testimony that the subject of algebra is truly a fascination here in La Paz. Mathematics was never my favorite subject in school, and so I ask the waiter to bring a candle to my table so that I have enough light to write in my journal. I remain there for hours, hazily drifting between musings of giant frogs and "a(b+c)=ab+ac."

. . .

It is 6AM and a pack of wild dogs are following me down to the lake. "Always carry a stick," I was advised, but these words seemed quite ludicrous to me at the time. This morning, I awakened at 4:45am in order to be down at the docks by sunrise for the first boat out to "Isla del Sol," the Island of the Sun that marks the birthplace of the first Sun God in mythological lore. My thinking was that I would be one step ahead if I arrived before the onslaught of tourists, but when I get there, not a single boat is to be seen. Instead, I am greeted by the frightening sight of a pack of wild dogs galloping towards me in a body language determined for its target. Feeling my shoulders tense, I stare straight ahead and proceed on tiptoe—like walking on eggs, while pretending to be calm and never turning around to meet their eyes. A small animal of some sort, perhaps a rabbit, runs past me. As luck would have it, this catches the attention of the hungry-for-breakfast scavengers and distracts them. I am massively relieved when the pack is diverted and chases their newfound prey up over a hill, to the right of me. In a single glance backwards, I turn to count their number, if only to confirm for my personal record just how large a gangly crew they actually were. I count nine dogs in all.

It is bitter cold at 6am. Between the high elevation of the Altiplano and the lack of a windbreak, the chill is unforgiving. Change of plans. I return to my room at the Playa Azul, bury my head in a pillow and go back to sleep. Misinformation, frustration and delay go hand in hand in the crooked path of travel. The wrong time, the missed boat, the unforeseen obstacle . . . these are the setbacks of our peregrinations whose memories are later mollified by the strong points of our adventure. Once returned home to the ordinariness of routine, our hardships become diminished in our recollection by the strength of gratitude we feel for having had an authentic experience. So when I arise at 8am for a second try and discover to my great dismay that a boat has already launched for Isla del Sol at 7:30am—I remind myself of this. Now, I will have to wait another few days for tourists to arrive in order to gather up a group of at least six passengers to rent a boat. I spend the rest of the morning in promenade, inspecting every nook and cranny of Copacabana city. With the exception of a stray llama and a few scattered sheep, there are few living beings around.

When three long days later, the one o'clock bus arrives from La Paz, I am elated to see passengers disembark. I hear a familiar voice.

"Can you help me with my luggage, young man?" To my astonishment, it is Toni, the Peace Corp worker I met in La Paz, soliciting help with her luggage. It is another one of Toni's endearing quirks that she travels with four huge suitcases, the sum of which are impossible for her to carry all at once.

"Toni, over here!" I yell, surprised to see that she has left La Paz so early. "What are you doing here?"

A huge grin crosses her face at the sight of me. "Sandy had to fly back to Lima yesterday," Toni explains. "She developed a sharp increase in blood pressure and had to get to a lower altitude as soon as possible. I decided to move on rather than stay in La Paz by myself."

Toni introduces me to her luggage carrier, Nick, a doctor from London who is making a brief lunch stop in Copacabana before he continues on to Puno. A blond man of delicate features and of an equally delicate English accent, Nick is a medic as well as a gracious lunch companion. He assures us that with rest and medication, Sandy will be just fine. "It was fortunate that she noticed the early danger signs before her condition became more serious," he says. After a light lunch of mineral water and ceviche, the raw marinated shrimp so deliciously prepared by the locals, we wave Nick off as he boards the afternoon bus to Puno, having unsuccessfully persuaded him to stay for the boat ride to Isla Del Sol. Toni and I split in separate directions, on a mission to find passengers for the boat.

Scouting the waterfront, I find Jacob and Isabella, a young couple from Brazil,. They are slim and tan and beautiful and are very interested in an excursion to Isla del Sol. So is Hal, a tourist from Germany, who, shirtless in his cut-off jeans and tattoos, could easily pass as a surfer from Southern California. Toni hunts down his girlfriend Marta, who hails from Switzerland, and convinces her to join us, in spite of the fact that Marta is not very fond of boats. With six people now in tow, we confirm our reservation for the first boat out tomorrow morning.

10

FOOT-TRAILS, PENANCE, AND REWARD

The fact that our driver is bailing buckets of water from the bottom of our boat is not a good sign. Neither is the black smoke wafting out from the overheated engine. By the time we reach Isla del Sol, that sacred place in Inca mythology equivocated to the Garden of Eden, we are all feeling queasy. Marta throws up off the side of the boat, as Hal lies beside her fast asleep, lulled by the seesaw of the rocking waves. Toni sits upright, fists planted to her waist, performing breathing exercises to combat her nausea. We had never considered getting seasick on our grand excursion.

At the northwest end of the island is the most sacred of stone huacas. At one time covered entirely in a layer of gold plate, its position marks the birthplace of the first Sun God. To the Incas, this peculiar mound of granite, which looks as if it is in the process of emerging from the ground, signifies the presence of a living spirit. Denoted in the Quechua language as a "huaca," otherwise spelled wak'a, any unusual aberration of nature, i.e., an odd-shaped stone, tree, or even a potato, designates the abode of a great divinity in material form. One may make the implication that in the rarity of the peculiar to the norm, the sacred was recognized and made worthy of attention. At the location of a huaca, a special carving or offering may often be found nearby.

A network of foot-trails crisscrosses over the island. Perhaps they are the faded pathways of the Sapa Incas who made their annual pilgrimage from Cusco to ask for a bountiful harvest. A series of steps lead directly into the water. One wonders for what objective these steps were arranged. Are they symbolic or purposeful? Possibly, they represent the footpath of the Creator-God Viracocha who disappeared into the waves of the lake in a splash of foam, earning the name Viracocha, for "foam of the sea."

I'm told that the best of the Inca artifacts are on the south side of the island, but it is impossible to persuade the boatman to go further. All of us sunburned, seasick, and unnerved by a leaky boat, we do not argue the point. Also off limits to us is the neighboring Island of the Moon (*Isla del Luna*), the birthplace of Mama Occlo, the female companion to the Sun God. Storied in antiquity as the anointed place where Virachocha invoked the rising of the moon, remnants of the "Palace of the Vestal Virgins" and "Temple to the Moon Mother" remain unseen by most visitors.

Fantastical rumors about Lake Titicaca abound. The locals give an intriguing account of subterranean cities hidden deep beneath the waters and many boatmen claim that when levels are low, they can actually touch the rooftops of ancient buildings with the tips of their oars. These beliefs are encouraged by Inca creation myths propagandizing the existence of a submerged city from which radiates a network of underground tunnels leading to Cusco. In the 1970s, such notions were bolstered when a diving team came upon the sunken remains of a metropolis below the eastern shores of the lake. It is conceivable that this rediscovered city had once been built in the wake of a long drought when lake waters were receded— then subsequently flooded over as the great rains returned.

Based on this word-of-mouth, the French oceanographer and explorer, Jacques Cousteau set off on a filmed expedition to search the depths of the 1,500 foot deep lake. Cousteau never found signs of a hidden city, although it was impossible to survey the entire square footage. However, what he did stumble upon during his investigation were the celebrated foot-long frogs of Titicaca that are distinguished to this region. All day I've searched for them with my binoculars, but I haven't seen a one. Nor have I heard the raucous chorus of croaking that is described as being loud enough to hear clear across to my hotel room in the evening. Not a ribbit.

Afternoon finds Toni and I hiking "Cerro Calvario," the Hill of Calvary overlooking the city of Copacabana, where the "Fourteen Stations of the Cross," representing the route of the "Via Crucis" that Jesus trod on his path to crucifixion, leads to a shrine of the

71

Holy Sepulchre at the top. Many before us do penance on their knees to the Sepulchre that symbolizes that most sacred of places to Christians, where Jesus was buried and resurrected. On holy days, such as Good Friday, virtually all of the townspeople who are devout Catholics will make their way up this path of sorrows to the summit. It is a punishing climb in the rarified air.

One by one, we pass a series of crosses, planted in their boxy concrete foundations. Some of them sport bronze plaques denoting contributions from wealthy benefactors, and all are scrawled with graffiti; those intrusive marks of personal identity that compel the passerby to render their temporal presence as immortal, alongside deserving almsgivers. Anticipating the main shrine at the top, a stunningly beautiful series of monuments form a consecutive line of arched encasements illustrating scenes from the fourteen stations of Christ's sufferings; each of the hulled chambers dropping bowed shadows upon each other in the falling sun. Below us, the sleepy village of Copacabana nestles peacefully in its valley, cushioned by moss-padded hills and the ever-pervasive mirrored lake whose enormity is now fully recognizable from these heights. It is an understated sunset, notable for its lack of color; the pure white rays glaring in all directions over the silver grey waters of dusk.

As we advance towards the final debilitating feet of our ascent, it is to our great amusement that we spot a young boy, positioned directly at the crowning point of our climb, selling plastic souvenirs in likeness of the Holy Sepulchre. At first, we are a bit taken aback at our tawdry prize for suffering, but moments later are rewarded for our grueling act of penance when a traveler from Germany, who has just returned from Cusco, informs us that the train strike is over.

11
STARRY SKIES AND FLOATING ISLANDS

It was all I could do to restrain myself. "No mas musica!" I so boldly shouted from my seat at the rear row, corner window of the bus. After three hours, I had had my fill of the rock n' roll travelling music blasting from the speakers on the bus ride from Copacabana to Puno. I guess it was unrealistic of me to expect indigenous flute music or perhaps a lovely *harawi* tune of soft lament to accompany our drive. As all eyes turn towards me aghast, I shrink down into my seat to escape their glare. I hide my face out the open window and lose myself in passing fields where rustic shacks built from soft-baked bricks of dung, earth, and straw stretch the line of view. Capped with roofs of corrugated tin, they are almost picturesque against the backdrop of Titicaca's basin, which we have already driven halfway around. I can finally see a few balsa reed boats.

From the front of the bus drift the chatty persuasions of Toni, as she befriends another strong-armed young man. One doesn't require psychic powers to predict that he is about to become her next Sherpa. When a border sign signals that we are crossing the threshold to Peru, I envisage warm waves of healing power running through my body, as if the very ground we tread on has a transformative quality from the Bolivia left behind. This morning, we had in fact departed Copacabana to the sendoff of an ear-splitting clap of thunder; the presage of a black storm to come. But I am jolted from such imaginings as the sight of the cold hard streets of Puno sends a sobering tug of recognition to my gut. It is noisy, dark and dirty. Conditions here look rough. Poised on the southwest edge of Lake Titicaca, this main port was established in 1668 as an important capital on the silver mining trail and is now the crossroads of train and bus transportation for travelers to and from Cusco, Arequipa, and La Paz. A mecca for tourists—and the street peddlers, innkeepers and restaurants that service them, Puno is also a vortex for the hustlers and pickpockets that exploit. Initiatory words of caution flash by my window, as we roll in: "Don't Be Careful, Be Paranoid" pronounces one sign posted over a cambio.

As I disembark the bus, an onslaught of barracudas take aim for their prey. Aggressive street peddlers push t-shirts and sweaters in my face, self-appointed travel agents try to lead me to their pensione, and hombres that can only be up to no good knock into me, brushing up against my arm and luggage. With a population of 100,000 people, I think to myself that most of them must be right here on these crowded streets. Toni and I have already agreed that we will stay here only long enough to visit the floating islands of the Uros Indians, study the balsa reed boats of the lake, and then move onwards to our destination of Machu Picchu.

Stefan, the amiable gentleman carrying two of Toni's suitcases is an astronomer from Stockholm, Sweden (an advantageous occupation in view of the timely appearance of Halley's Comet). Quite slim and lanky, with a ball of fuzzy brown hair atop his head, he sports an equally fuzzy red mustache with a rather tired handlebar, drooping at each end. His body language cuts a somewhat flamboyant posture, along with what appears to be a permanent twinkle stuck in his eye—a look of the debonair that says any day could be his lucky day.

Stefan has arrived straight from Chile, where for five weeks he has been observing spots on stars at the Cerro Tololo Inter-American Observatory in the high desert, east of La Serena. At dinner, we bombard him with a litany of questions. It's our chance to ask everything we've always wanted to ask about astronomy, and more. Fortunately, Stephan doesn't seem to mind, answering all our queries in a clear concise vocabulary, accessible to the layman. Toni and I focus in our attention, mesmerized by the paper napkin on which Stefan takes pen to draw a diagram of the solar system. Upon this ordinary paper napkin are delineated the fathomless cosmos of Einstein's Theory of Relativity, and the enigmatic conundrum of the Black Hole. Supernovas and comets, the moons of Jupiter, and the course of Voyagers I and II continue along the rim of a paper plate.

When the waiter brings the bill, the cost of our inexpensive dinner confounds us. Between three persons, we have consumed five Pisco Sours, two espressos, two soups, one spaghetti and two chicken dinners, with ice cream for desert. The check for all this food and drink amounts to a mere grand total of nine American dollars, with tax and tip included. When the waiter brings our change, he gives us a coin that has become so de-valued that it is of minus monetary worth. "Negative mass," Stefan chuckles, pocketing it as a souvenir.

On the walk back to our two-dollar per night pensione, the astronomy lesson continues. Convening on the fourth floor terrace for a view of the celestial heavens, Stefan demonstrates the correct way to observe stars indirectly, instead of head on, by staring past them so that the curve of the eye can take in more light (a trick when looking through a telescope). In these clear skies of the southern hemisphere, the luminous swirl of the Milky Way is a ghostly apparition; its three hundred trillion stars of gas and dust so aptly named as "Mayu" (The River) by the Incas. As a guidepost that held enormous importance for the Inca, it was from this spiraled galaxy of planets and stars that critical delineations of time and space were calculated. Having taken note of the tilted angle of the Milky Way, positioned upwards from left to right for part of the year, then right to left for the second part, Inca astronomers envisioned imaginary lines that crossed the night sky and dissected at angles. From these lineaments were conceived the four pie-shaped quadrants called *suyu*, correlating to a Northeast-Southwest and Southeast-Northwest navigational map, enabling the Incas to predict weather and seasonal change as they tracked the movement of stars across the quadrants. This visionary mapping of the cosmos may have become the framework for the structure of the Inca empire itself, as notably, the four quarters of the Inca empire, named respectively Chinchaysuyu, Antisuyu, Collasuyu, and Cuntisuyu, carry the nomenclature *suyu*.

Stefan pinpoints the belt of Orion and the Seven Sisters of the cobalt blue Pleiades, on display in all their majesty. I consider that the stars I now gaze upon are the very same stars that the Incas worshipped as secondary deities, paying homage to their light with a Chapel to the Pleiades (called *Kolka* in Quechua) within the Temple of the Sun in Cusco. The enormous disc that formed the central core of the sun temple was the locus for a series of radiating lines divided and reduced from quadrants into finer ceques, emulating the rays of the sun. Historians conjecture that this sun dial was not solely a calendar of light and shadow, but a cosmic barometer that tracked the cycle of the Pleiades, as well as the all-important planet/star Venus, so-named *Chasca*, or "the youth with the long and curling locks" by the Incas, who identified this attendant to the Sun God for the beauty of its nature, as well as the changing seasons.

. . .

The Uros Indians, who live exclusively on the floating reed islands of Lake Titicaca, are an intransigent culture that has survived both Aymara and Inca domination. Once a noble fishing tribe and the self-anointed caretakers of the lake, the Uros were regarded as so poor and of such crude living standards, that the Incas considered them beings of subhuman proportion. Although no pure Uros native exists today, this small population of three to four hundred individuals inhabits over forty islands of the lake, maintaining centuries of ancestral tradition.

Arriving via a small motorboat that we have rented at the jetty in Puno, we step foot on the floating island of Huacavacani, where a handful of children run to greet us. They tug at my hand and yank my sweater, looking for candy and small gifts, but for the moment I am preoccupied with the ground beneath my feet, or should I say the reeds beneath my feet. Created entirely from layers of piled *tortora reeds*, these islands are literally floating rafts upon the open waters. As I take each deliberate step forward onto the spongy surface, I can hear my feet make squishy sounds as they spring with the give and take of the reed floor moving under me. These wheat-yellow tortora reeds, a variety of the balsa (Spanish for "something that floats") are known for the usefulness of their pliability, as well as for their buoyancy. Gathered almost daily from the lush perimeters of the lake, these reeds are the mainstay of life for the Uros Indians who build their houses, boats and islands from this bountiful gift of Titicaca. Over forty man-made reed islands can be found floating upon the lake at any given time, the largest of these being Toranipata, Santa Maria, and the island where we now woozily stand, Huacavacani.

A small boy chatters excitedly as he leads me towards a cluster of exquisite reed huts. They are crafted wholly from bundles of golden tortora, wrapped and bound together in the most graceful of contours. Each hut is singular in character each from the other. Their organic figures of oscillating arcs twist and bend, sculpted by the course of an unremitting wind as a bonsai tree is shaped by its cordage. Three native women sit squat in front of them, composing a freeze-frame postcard for our eyes as they weave orange and yellow striped wall hangings and miniature replicas of balsa reed boats. Others of them go about their daily chores, cooking, cleaning, and minding the children, dispassionate to our arrival. I'm cognizant that they may be poised for display of the tourist trade, however it still seems a bit disconcerting to observe them so closely, as if they are a human exhibition of sorts. I find myself wondering how it is they keep warm, and if fire must be a constant worry. What happens when it rains? And do the islands ever float away or sink?

"Over here," calls Stefan. "You have to see this!" To our surprise, a Seventh Day Adventist Mission School (made of reeds, of course) has managed to establish itself on the island. Crudely simplistic and of the most minimalist construction, it is topped at the A-frame with a large wooden cross. Inside, a green blackboard hangs from the wall and thumb-worn schoolbooks lie open on the ground; the evidence of an active classroom and its students. Perhaps, lessons are in recess and the children will be back any time now.

My expectations of seeing a balsa reed boat are surpassed when I get to take a ride on one. At first, I balk at the prospect when I see the nine-year old boy who will be my gondolier. "Race ya to the island!" shouts Toni—and at that I realize that Toni and Stefan have already taken off ahead of me on another boat. Now I alone, will ride with the nine-year old boy as my oarsman on a cruise from one island to the next.

Of such resplendent form and line, this canoe-like craft, whose likeness has sailed the ocean from North Africa to the Americas, is constructed by the lashing together of four long bundles of reeds in a seafaring design that is a centuries old custom. Sometimes hastened by a reed sail made of paper-thin pulp, most often, as today, only a single set of oars is required to direct its course. Such a lovely sight it is; the unadorned plushness of its amber-gold weave intensified against the stark blue waters and the clear blue sky.

As I climb aboard the vessel, I am reassured of my designated boatman's abilities when I come to see the surprising power he packs in his child-sized arms. Thrusting the boat into the lake with a burst of gusto, he handily asserts his place at the oars and is apparently more than capable enough to deliver me to my destination safely. "What is your name?" I inquire of the young boy with whom I will now trust with my life and well-being. "My name is Pablito," he replies with spunky enthusiasm. "We go now!"

Like a swan skimming cool waters, our movement across the lake is smooth and effortless, with a serene and fluid motion that renders the wake left behind us as almost imperceptible. The sturdiness of the reed boat surprises me, so much so that I feel secure enough to lie back and enjoy the experience. Closing my eyes, I can feel the muscles in my arms unclench; my shoulders slacken and relax. I am gliding on ice. I am floating on glass. It is heaven.

No sooner do we pull up to shore at the next island than I stumble over a soft spot in the flooring. Faster than stepping into quicksand, my entire left foot sinks in clear down to my ankle. "Let me help you, Senorita." The source of the voice is the captain of the motorboat we rented in Puno. Supporting my arm by the elbow, he holds me steadily and leans his body against mine. His right arm comes uncomfortably close to my bosom. I had ignored Captain Herve's stares for the duration of the boat ride to Huacavacani, but now I am pressed to be on guard as he smiles a toothy grin and positions his face very close to mine. "Captain Herve is always here to help you," he says.

The soft spot I've fallen into is one of the drawbacks that make maintaining the islands an endlessly laborious task. As the bottom-most reeds of the floating platforms decay very rapidly, the top layers need to be constantly replaced. Barring this, the only other threats to life on the islands are the annual rains with its rising floodwaters, and the lure of the mainland with its electricity, televisions and discos. To a great extent, the Uros have achieved the dreams of many. Never having to pay a bill or punch a time clock, they live entirely off the natural environment, which provides sustenance of food, shelter and habitat. Fishermen by trade, the daily catch supplies the required nutrients of proteins and oils, with the remainder bartered for fresh produce on the mainland. Like a colony of birds assembling their nests, the Uros build and re-build their homes, boats, and the very ground they walk on, bobbing unanchored like nomads on a body of water fifteen times the size of Lake Geneva. Living off the bounties of nature, it seems to be an idyllic life, but is it really?

By six o'clock, we are back on the motorboat returning to Puno. Toni and Stefan compare cameras and lenses while I sit apart silently, relishing what may be my last view of Titicaca. Gradually, I become aware of a stare upon my person. When I look up, it is none other than Captain Herve gawking with fixed gaze upon my toes protruding from the tips of my brown leather sandals. He is smiling that wide toothy grin again. When I turn to acknowledge that I have noticed his fixation, he tips his cap and winks at me, then re-focuses back on my toes, which I try my best not to wiggle. I begin to suspect that he has a foot fetish and is perhaps getting his jollies by eyeing a bit of flesh, but I convince myself that he's probably admiring my footwear instead . . . perhaps wondering where I purchased my sandals?

Exhausted from the daylong excursion, Toni, Stefan and I retire to our individual rooms to take a nap before dinner. I kick my shoes off and stretch out on the bed, attempting to re-image myself floating on that lovely balsa reed boat . . . the sky, the mirrored lake, the tranquil glide . . . then suddenly . . . a knock at the door. Thinking it must be room service; I swing the door open without hesitation, only to find none other than Captain Herve standing at my threshold.

"Buenos Noches, Senorita, may I come in?"

I am very taken aback. How did he know what hotel I'm staying in? And how did he get my room number? Furthermore, why did the front desk not announce him? The old New Yorker self-protective instinct kicks in. It occurs to me that he could force his way into my room and no one would ever know. I get a bad feeling.

Captain Herve beams his pearly whites, a near perfect set of straight shiny white teeth. He is staring directly down at my bare feet.

"I'm waiting for my husband, who will arrive tonight from Lima," I lie spontaneously, and then slam the door shut, adding . . . "and he is a very jealous man!"

That night I sleep with my portable door jam on.

12
THE WAY TO

The early morning train out of Puno departs for Cusco at 6:30am with an estimated time of arrival, twelve hours later. Our journey will take us across the grassy plains of the Lake District, past the market towns of Juliaca and Ayaviri, and through the mountains of the La Raya Pass before our final descent into the Vilcanota Valley.

The scene at the train station is a clamor of waving arms and shouts, pushing and shoving; anxiety-ridden passengers with too much luggage; smoke and the smell of fuel burning; peddlers selling one last trinket. A film of dust mixes with the air, burning my eyes. Forbidding storm clouds darken the light of day, passive to our struggle. A battle ensues for the open doors of the train, and in the scramble of mass confusion, Toni, Stefan and I manage to keep within eyesight of each other. Stefan hops aboard first, grabbing a pair of facing seats by a window, with a much coveted folding table in-between. I stow my overnight bag under a seat while Stefan stuffs his knapsack and two of Toni's suitcases in an overhead bin. The rest of Toni's luggage blocks the aisle, sending the exasperated passengers who have to climb over it into a barrage of disgruntled protestations. "Who the hell do these suitcases belong to?" yells one angry tourist.

Disquiet turns to calm as the train whistle blows and we begin to move. Outside the safe haven of our compartment, overcast skies transform the colors of the landscape into somber shades of gray. It begins to rain. Toni amuses herself by playing Solitaire with a deck of Snoopy cards, laying out the faces of Charlie Brown, Lucy and Peanuts on the plastic folding table. Stefan shows a little boy how to find Sweden on a map. But soon, we have all dozed off, tranquilized by the chugging motion of the train and the parting sight of the Lake District.

In the heart of a traveler, a train ride, or any ride, for that matter, is never merely a means of getting from point *a* to point *b*. It is the lure of the road, the path, and the way to that is itself the fascination. Within the self-contained existence of our train car or bus, we stumble upon the lives of our fellow travelers whom destiny has coupled with us. Together as strangers we make passage upon "the places in-between," affording ourselves the opportunity to steal a glimpse into the lives of those we pass by so fleetingly, and whom we shall never see again.

Once, when traveling in Japan, I boarded the wrong train. "Does the train to Hikone depart from this track?" I had asked of a kindly old gentleman, in my practiced Japanese phonetics. I had had strict instructions from friends that I should always ask the open question in Japan—never ask, is this the right track, or is this the right train? Japanese etiquette dictates that it is not polite to correct another person if they are mistaken, so consequently, no one would tell me if I was amiss. Feeling confident that I had asked my question properly and had received the correct answer, I boarded the first train that arrived. But something went terribly wrong. What I didn't know was that numerous trains to varied destinations shared the same track. As the train climbed higher and the landscape began rising into mountainous slopes, I realized that I was going in the wrong direction—hopelessly lost and unable to turn back on an express train that wouldn't come to a stop for over two hours. Unable to read Hiragana, the calligraphy characters on the signs that buzzed past me out the window, I had no idea where I was going. There was no point of reference in the English or Latin languages that I could puzzle. I could not pronounce the symbols that I saw, nor could I speak them. "Where am I?" I wondered. Powerless to change what I could not change, I resigned to accept my fate. Burrowing my back into a comfortable corner of the soft-padded seat, I settled myself down to look at the view. Outside my window, the cluttered skyline of the city had exploded to the open skies. A patchwork of glimmering rice paddies, saturated in pools of shallow water, pulsated in delicate shadows of mirrored light. The hilltops, as electric green as the neon of Tokyo, became dotted with timbered buildings and farms. I was a traveler, exploring a place that I didn't know. What did it matter that I was going the wrong way? A visceral sensation swept over me; something akin to the thrill of an adventure and a confidence in the unknown that was to come. I didn't think back, and I didn't think forward. I stayed present in the experience of where I was, and I never took my eyes off the window view. It was the most beautiful countryside I had ever seen in Japan, and I relished every moment.

Eventually, I made it to Hikone that day. When I was finally able to get off the train, I returned to my starting point, taking extra precaution to ask my directions properly. To this day, I have no idea where I had been on that most memorable train ride in Japan, but I was never to forget it. Perhaps, the real grist of travel is the life that exists between our points of destination as a destination unto itself. Travel for the sake of travel. Motion for the sake of motion.

When in an hour, we make a brief stop at the Juliaca station to pick up more passengers; it results in a whirlwind of activity from the Quechua natives who have set up shop along the rails. In a frenetic game of Beat the Clock, they dangle jewelry, trinkets and snacks in a last ditch sales effort to close a bargain before the train departs. From out the window of the train, Toni bargains down six alpaca sweaters and Stefan samples a cup of orange soup served from a steaming black vat. An old Quechua man, who didn't want his photo taken, throws a rotten mango at Toni's head. We all burst into fits of laughter. Stefan points out the tiniest baby girl lying on the ground, swaddled in a thick white bundle of cloth. Her brother, a child himself, picks her up and flings her over his back, and then like a magician using slight of hand, he creates an instant papoose with just a few quick flicks of the wrist. Among the new passengers boarding the train are Bill and Sharon, the backpackers from Australia that we first met in La Paz. They spot us instantly and join our train car. For a time, we sit together in stillness, just taking it all in; the voices, the colors, the faces—the experience of Peru.

. . .

83

Bill and Sharon are very annoyed with me. Energized by our climatic arrival in Cusco, I suggested that we could easily walk to our hotel from the train station, instead of waiting for a taxi. Although the walk couldn't have been more than a third of a mile, Bill, in particular, is really incensed. He is tired from the twelve-hour train ride and becomes agitated after only walking a few blocks. This is very surprising to me, in view of the fact that he is a backpacker who is hiking his way across South America. His Australian accent turns from charming to brittle when he loses his temper, "This is too far to walk, damn it!"

Returning to the hacienda of Los Marqueses feels like a homecoming. The rich mahogany paneling and ornately carved doors, of which I have become intimately familiar, are no longer solely a remembrance in my mind's eye. New flowers of purple lace bloom through the wrought iron gates and freshly polished windows sparkle with the scent of fresh lemon. Arroya, the talkative green parrot who makes its home in the courtyard, greets us with an "Ola!" When Toni answers back in a voice mimicking the high-pitched shriek of the bird, an unsuspecting gentleman exiting his room responds "Ola!" All five of us break into rolls of laughter, giddy with relief from the tense moments, just earlier.

Our dinner at La Trattoria turns into an evening of celebration when we learn that Sandy has arrived in Cusco, compounded by running into Nick, the doctor from London, who we come upon sitting alone. We celebrate Sandy's improved health and Nick's last night in the Andes. He is on his way to the Amazon rainforest, where he'll stay at a facility run by an American anthropologist.

"He's got two lodges and one camping ground, each of them deeper than the next into primary jungle," gushes Nick. "Its still uncharted territory out there. Imagine over four thousand species of birds, two thousand species of fish, sixty species of reptile, and so many insects that scientists can't even classify them!"

"Not to mention the pink porpoises!" I chime in, enamored by the thought of the massive jungle, a primeval forest covering an area over seven million square kilometers, which remains as much a subject of mystery as it was hundreds of years ago. Sharing borderlands with Brazil and Peru, the bulk of the rainforest spills into Brazil, with thirteen percent of it in Peru. For any impassioned explorer of South America, the twisting course of the Amazon River and its tributaries offers one more portal into unknown territory. With the presence of an astronomer in our midst, the conversation once again turns to the celestial skies. Stefan presides over a question and answer session about Halley's Comet that holds the attention of everyone in the restaurant. Two travelers from Spain, who are sitting at the next table, draw their chairs closer, and even the waiters listen in, tiptoeing quietly around us as they serve our colas.

When after dinner, I meander through the labyrinthine alleyways of Cusco, I do so with no particular destination in mind. Around each turn comes new disclosure: a freshly painted flower box, an elaborate wood-carved balcony, and another Inca wall of puzzled blocks; bringing to mind the Japanese aesthetic *miegakure*, the hide-and-reveal technique of the visible and invisible used in Japanese gardening. By design, the pathway through a Japanese garden is never straightforward and is otherwise laid out so as not to exhibit the garden all at once. One is intentionally led to slow down and wander without hurry through a winding trail that discloses only bits and pieces of the garden at any one time; a red-leafed maple tree; a gurgling fountain; a grey stone lantern. We are resultantly surprised at every bend and may relish each new detail with delight for what comes unexpectedly, as the hidden lays bare.

Around such a bend of miegakure, I turn to discover a neighborhood market where the animated chatter of street vendors ensconced in the livelihood of bargaining, takes precedence over the night. Here, in the clearing of a small plaza, the dark of the evening is lit by the glow of an open fire pit where a huge kettle of fish-stew simmers. Quechua women roast the potatoes called chunyos of the most remarkable shapes and colors; their seasoned aroma wafting in the dense smoky air. Raw carcasses of meat hang from their posts, ready for slicing; canvas sacks brim over with corn kernels and coffee beans; and fruit stalls are piled high with melons, mangoes, and bananas. It is a glimpse inside a secret world to the true life of its residents after the hordes of tourists have turned in for the evening—the invisible now visible.

13

LIKE THE GREAT WINGS OF A CONDOR

That which was deemed to be lost
was never lost,
But remaining all the long while
to be revealed.

In 1911, Hiram Bingham III, Yale Professor and future Connecticut
State Senator, set forth on an expedition to Peru in pursuit of the
legendary Lost City of the Incas. Somewhat like the story of the man
in "The Roads of Life" who was determined to find the source of the
sound he heard, Bingham followed a calling, embarking on his quest
with marked singularity of purpose. Enlisting the help of local
campesinos, he was to withstand a series of perilous ventures before
he would meet his reward. Scaling the heights of dizzying cliffs,
crawling through viper infested mud, and negotiating raging rapids,
he too, would search in all directions, stumbling over boulders and
falling into ditches at every wrong turn. And just like the man in
Dinesen's childhood tale, Bingham remained undaunted in the face
of all obstacles before he would be recompensed by light of day with
a most breathtaking discovery. Hidden high upon a ridge, two
thousand feet above the Rio Urumbamba, and cloistered by the
cloud forest for whose imagery the indigenous peoples have
bynamed the "Ceja de la Selva" (*The Jungle's Eyebrow*), sat a
magnificent citadel of stone. Camouflaged by the natural defenses of
the neighboring mountain range, which for centuries had rendered
it virtually invisible from below, a lost kingdom stood draped
beneath a tangled overgrowth of tropical forest. Waiting to be
unearthed were the royal quarters of an Inca King, a Sun Temple, a
House of the Chosen Women, residences, agricultural terraces, and
over one hundred flights of steps prototypical of Inca city planners.
For Hiram Bingham, the hardships of his journey were at once
superseded, and then vanquished, by the gift of his prize. In the rest

of his long and prosperous life, nothing would compare with this moment. Naming the place Machu Picchu (*Old Peak*) after the larger of two peaks overlooking the city, he declared it to be the infamous "Lost City of the Incas."

Today, most historians dispute these claims, believing the ruins at the less picturesque Espiritu Pampa, a settlement that Bingham himself had previously explored, to be the last stronghold of the Incas. A 1964 excavation of Espiritu Pampa, whose location fits the profile as chronicled in historical records of that era, revealed an extensive compound with over sixty buildings, three hundred homes, temples of worship, plazas and waterways. In reality, none of the so-called experts have ever been able to prove their claims to a certainty. Many contest this new theory and continue to support Bingham's interpretation of the facts. What does remain forever unchallenged in Hiram Bingham's remarkable discovery is that Machu Picchu is one of the most important archaeological finds of the century. A sacred huaca of major significance to the Incas, this was an intentionally hidden city, preserved in all its glory and never to be exploited by the Spanish invaders.

The train to Machu Picchu is scheduled to depart the San Pedro Station at 7am sharp. Toni and the others have decided to stay on in Cusco, while Stefan and I are moving ahead, anxious to get to the ruin site as soon as possible. Most tourists who make the seventy-five mile journey to Machu Picchu on a pre-packaged tour will arrive at their destination by 11am, spend a few hours there and then return to Cusco same-day, via the 3pm train. They are so-called the "day-trippers" for what is more accurately just a few hours. To day-trip is to deprive oneself of the experience of exploring the ruins in detail and to remain there in solitude after the crowds have gone. I plan to base myself at the nearby town of Aquas Caliente with an open-ended schedule, while Stephan is pressed to head home tomorrow.

Our seats are positioned on the left-hand side of the train, just as I planned it. Here's where the best views are, according to my guidebook. I glance over at Stefan, who appears a bit distant this morning. He seems inside himself, deep within his thoughts. I do not intrude. I observe him as he devours his daily dose of potassium, a breakfast of two ripe bananas, in all of ten seconds, as I counter by downing a few cherry cough drops for sustenance. When the train begins to move, my eyes well up with tears. Why did it mean so much to me, this hidden city, so deep in the jungle? What was I projecting onto this Inca sanctuary, so mysterious, so surrounded by beauty? An American woman initiates a conversation. "I'm from Chicago. Where are you from?" she asks. But I do not want to chat. I am on my way to Machu Picchu and I want to savor every moment.

First up, and then back down again, the train engages in a series of switchbacks from right to left, alternately gaining elevation and then losing it in a repetitive zigzag pattern that ironically mimics the crooked footpaths characteristic to the Inca. This will continue for some minutes before our final descent into the Sacred Valley. At 8,000 feet, Machu Picchu is actually lower in elevation than Cusco at 11,200 feet, but most visitors will have the false impression of having climbed higher, due to the switchbacks. The train whistle blows and we push forward. Another whistle and we backtrack down, and then up again—I'd say about seven times, although I didn't really count. The train is crawling along very slowly at these turns and passengers begin to get drowsy. When we gradually pick up speed, I head for the rear of the compartment to shoot photographs out the large picture window. As we emerge from a tunnel, I snap a few frames as the train maneuvers around some spectacular bends that are all-inclusive of mountains, tracks, river and sky. Soon, the scenery becomes dramatic. The hills grow lush, dense with foliage, and wild with a blanket of mossy growth. Amidst the greenery that zooms by appear spots of color; Andean wildflowers of vibrant yellow and red, and a fleeting carpet of the pink and orange orchids known as *wiñay wayna* that steals my breath away. The Romanesque peaks of the Andes rise above us in their ever-imposing wise way; their benevolent soft lines conceding nary a jagged edge.

When I rejoin Stefan in our seats, I find him mesmerized at the windowpane, unable to break his lock on the view. "I can hardly believe my eyes," he says. Our train has joined the snake of the Urubamba River, a crashing torrent of muddy brown waters hell bent on a speed course somewhere ahead of itself. First widening, then narrowing, the raging rapids crash over boulders that run into waterfalls, above and below, over and around. If we follow the twists and turns of this crooked course, surely it will lead us to a precious jewel.

"Look there!" A flash of snowy peaks. "And there!" Another. We are now alert with the eyes and ears of a cat about to pounce on its prey. Stefan reaches up to open a window. The thunder of the river swells into our compartment, amplifying its presence so that we can no longer hear ourselves speak over it without shouting. What sound. What energy. What power was here! Said Hiram Bingham of his first sight of this land:

> In the variety of its charms and the power of its spell, I know of no place in the world, which can compare with it. Not only has it great snow peaks looming above the clouds more than two miles overhead; gigantic precipices of many-colored granite rising sheer for thousands of feet above the foaming, glistening, roaring rapids; it has also, in striking contrast, orchids and tree ferns, the delectable beauty of luxurious vegetation, and the mysterious witchery of the jungle.[3]

The microbus ascending the z-lined trail above the Machu Picchu train station appears as minuscule as a child's toy, dwarfed by the heights of the two thousand foot cliff it scales. By the time we have exited the crowded train, we find ourselves at the end of a long queue of visitors waiting their turn to ride on one. Strangers bound together in a collective spirit of anticipation, we all gape skywards, rubbernecking for a view of the mini-bus as it climbs an arduous series of eighteen switchbacks before it reaches its destination. Somewhere over that ridge lies the lost city—but from our position below, there is no hint of it. It's easy to imagine how the Conquistadores would have missed it.

When the last bus returns from its happy mission of depositing its cargo of awestruck tourists at the site they will remember for the rest of their lives, it is at last our turn to board. We find the van to be equipped with expansive windows that pull in the view—and to our surprise, even the roof is made of glass. Hugging a wall of hillside thick with vegetation, our bus jostles up the rather bumpy dirt road, giving us a rambunctious ride that adds to the exhilaration of the experience. I soon realize why this is a van where every seat is arranged for the view—for there across the gorge from us lay a magnificent range of peaks, accentuated by the jaw-dropping sight of Putucusi at over 8500 feet. That Putucusi (Quechua for *Happy Mountain*) is regarded as an "apu" (holy mountain) is immediately conveyed by the sense of wind in your bones at the sheer sight of its titanic presence. In my dreamlike reverie, I can't help but imagine Putucusi as somehow human, posturing in a gesture that leans forward as if to whisper in the ear of a neighboring peak. Huddled together as if in commiseration, the assemblage of elephantine green figures that comprise the range appear to gather closely, as if ensconced in deep conversation. Ascending to the most towering of the adjacent cliffs, their rounded caps pierce translucent clouds of mist, fashioning them as soft crowns of lace upon their heads. There is no mistaking it now—we have entered unto the holy territory of the Inca.

Once off the bus, we need only walk a short footpath to arrive at the gate that leads to Machu Picchu. The other way to enter the grounds is as the Incas did centuries ago, via a four day, thirty-mile hike on the Inca Trail, leading to the "Intipunku," the Sun Gate, on the far end of the ruin site. Now past the Machu Picchu Hotel (the only hotel located at the site) and the Guard's Station, there is only a twist and turn remaining before we will enter the grounds, but even at such close proximity, I still see no trace of the city. The anticipation of this moment wells up inside me. All the planning, all the waiting, the obstacles and the detours have led me to this time and place—but first moments don't always happen as one expects. To my chagrin, conditions of the overcast day have created a whiteout of fog, veiling the entire view, and just as I brace myself for the first sight of Machu Picchu, my expectant state is deflated by a blanket of massive cloud cover.

"Where is it?" mumbles Stefan. "Are we here?

"The city of Machu Picchu covers a surface area over five square kilometers . . ." says a nearby tour guide, beginning his narrative on the finer details of the geographical coordinates, despite the non-appearance of its featured star.

I quickly revert to *Plan B*, having read about the postcard view seen from the Watchman's Hut. "I'm climbing to the Watchman's Hut, there, above the terraces." I motion to Stefan with a wave of my arm, but he doesn't follow.

It is along the first group of agricultural terraces to the left of us that a flight of stepped platforms lead to the Watchman's Hut, a lookout point where the iconic panorama of Machu Picchu that has been immortalized on magazines and tourist brochures, may be seen. In the few minutes it takes me to reach the viewing station at the top, the tropical mist has already dissipated, unmasking the city in all it's splendor. For an instant, the beauty stills my breath. It is a moment of aesthetic arrest.

Under the protective shadow of two sugarloaf pinnacles, the larger of the two-named Huayna Picchu (*Young Peak*), the citadel of Machu Picchu spills over a mound-like hemisphere gradating in stepped terraces down the hillside. Remnants of Inca structures, so generously preserved by time, suggest a mottled gray texture against the constancy of the wet, green turf. There seems to have been a mindfulness to the laws of nature here, as both city and horticulture are thoughtfully paired together in accordance with the elemental features of the landscape; completing the master plan of the Royals in an organic synergy. Permeating every inch of the 180-degree vista displayed before me, even the mountains of the Cordillera Reale participate in the picture scheme, providing a backdrop across the horizon from left to right for as far as the eye can see. From my lookout point at the Watchman's Hut, I imagine the peripheral slopes of Huayna Picchu and its companion peak as outstretched arms embracing the city below it in a protective posture, like the great wings of a condor hovering over its nest.

Choosing to spend my first moments alone in thought with Machu Picchu, I seat myself at the edge of a grassy landing and try to take it all in. Here, from the consummate vantage point prepared by Incas architects before me, I can spot the barrier wall that edges the southern region of the city, the open square of the sacred plaza, and the agricultural sector that is obvious to the eye from its numerous flights of terraces. At 8,038 feet, the municipality of Machu Picchu spans over 32,000 acres and contains over 140 structures, including residences, temples and sacred sites that are sectioned into three distinct precincts, so-designated by contemporary archaeologists as the Residential, the Sacred, and the Royal.

Recognizable to me for its distinct design is the "Intihuatana," the Sun Temple notable for its two-story curved wall indicating a shrine or holy temple of some sort. Nicknamed by Peruvians as *El Torréon* for its round medieval-style tower resembling that of a castle, its location at the heart of the city is another clue to its importance. A cavern below the structure houses a hollow chamber known as the Royal Mausoleum, complete with niches believed to have held the royal mummies. In contrast to the Egyptians, who permanently entombed their royals in preservation for the afterlife, the Incas re-dressed and cared for the corpses of their deceased kings, carrying them out to the main square to participate in ceremonial rites at Winter Solstice and other important anniversaries. Clothed in multicolored and finely woven garments; the intricacy of the weave emblematic of the stature of the royal king or priest, the former sovereigns were lovingly tended to by the Chosen Women, who draped their bodies with wildflowers as they were placed on their thrones and poised to watch the sun rise. The entire populace would gather to pay homage, entertaining with song, dance, and offerings of handcrafted gifts, food and chicha. The belief was held close that in exchange for these honorific acts, the royal ancestors would bestow blessings upon their worshippers, tending to the living as the living tended to the dead. Although the physical bodies of the former Sapa Incas had been transfigured through putrefaction, the domain of the Inca Sun God was deemed to be eternal and all the wiser to preside over important ritual. Such

SOMETHING LOST BEHIND THE RANGES

perspective is not unheard of in the annals of antiquity. Belief in the authority of ancestors to influence the fate of the living can be found from China to Japan to Africa, and have been traced as far back as Mesopotamia, third millennium BC.

I have been intrigued by photographs of an hourglass carved staircase inside the chamber of the Royal Mausoleum. It is my first stop. As I approach, an unusually somber tour group exits the Sun Temple, bestowing upon me the prize of solitude for my exploration.

"Which way is the mausoleum . . . with the staircase?" I ask, finding myself inquiring of the group as a whole, as I spontaneously draw an outline in the air.

"That way," respond two backpackers in unplanned unison, as if anticipating a familiar question.

Just within eyesight is the cavern named by Hiram Bingham as the *Royal Mausoleum* (or the Royal Tomb), containing a stairway leading to nowhere. Four steps of white granite, reflecting a pale dusty rose against the incandescence of daylight, reach to the ceiling of the now hollow chamber. Sculpted from a single sheet of bedrock, its billowing silhouette swells open at the center, as if exhaling a living breath. An hourglass section of fitted blocks, looking as if they have been wrung in the middle by two giant hands, are squeezed between the staircase and the adjoining wall. This unusual interplay of architecture to environment appears synchronized to the organic curvature of the cave, spurring a quizzical, even bewildered reaction from many. What was this special place? And what did it mean?

Now standing directly in front of the stairway, I slowly trace my fingers over the periphery of its edges the way I knew an Inca stone carver before me must have done, in a time so long ago. A master sculptor, he would have been, esteemed for his virtuous conduct, as well as for his artistry, in order to be entrusted with a task of such importance. Patiently, he must have hewn each arc of this stone in collaboration with the ways of its grain. Meticulously, he must have smoothed and polished every inch of it until the rutted surface was seamlessly fluent. As I run my hand along the contours of the stairs, I imagine how I follow in the path of its creator, who carved it with the tactile grace of hands that could see.

Is it possible this was a sacred stairwell to the heavens, the metaphoric steps for the spirits of deceased royals to climb to the realm of the gods, akin in purpose to the "ladders to heaven" characteristic of the American Indians of the Southwest? I remind myself that in order to understand the motivation of the Inca, one must always keep foremost in mind the extent to which the religious spirit infiltrated daily life. For the Incas, worship of the gods was a vital practice that influenced every action, including the farming of crops, the weaving of cloth, and the carving of stone. The Sun Temple is testimony to such an act. Despite the probability that the blocks of this tower were concealed under layers of plaster and decorative paint, with the finer aspects of the stonework unseen, every detail of the temple has been crafted to perfection. Without the use of adhesive mortar, or the hard forging tools of iron and steel, every block has been painstakingly fitted in a manner worthy of the gods. "The finer the stonework, the more important the building," I recant to myself, almost as if chanting a mantra inside my head.

A voice calls out from across the plaza. It is Stefan, looking and sounding as a different man from the one who accompanied me on the train here this morning. I make my way to him, climbing over a flight of steps to an area I recognize as the Royal Sector where Inca Kings, priests and their magistrates, once resided. Stefan catches up halfway at the Sacred Plaza, the religious center of the city. Together we explore the Temple of Three Windows, a rectangular structure distinguished by three trapezoidal windows facing out towards city and mountain views. The mildly bent persuasion of the vertical window frames and the rounded corners of the bottom sills are a clue to their significance; marking divergence from the linear lines of the functional to the nonlinear curves of the sacred. That there are three windows may speak of a triad, or allude to a story punctuated by three components or stages. Reinforcing this notion is the presence of a nearby stepping stone said to represent the three dimensions of existence: "Hanan-Pacha" (*heaven*), "Kay-Pacha" (*earth*) and "Ukju-Pacha" (*under-earth*). Hiram Bingham speculated that the three trapezoidal windows of this temple represented the creation caves of Inca mythology, but this is one of many theories that cannot be substantiated.

Nearby, the remnants of the Principal Temple enclose an enormous stone altar, over fourteen feet long. Positioned to overlook the expanse of the Sacred Plaza, one might imagine that important rituals to the creator-god Viracocha took place here. A pathway of steps leads to the Ornamental Chamber, a small but exquisite structure where long, flat terraces rise to the ridge of the Machu Picchu pinnacle, the sacred apu that is the namesake of the city. One may surmise that this chamber was built in complementarity to the Principal Temple, and was perhaps an antechamber of sorts where accessories used for the embellishment of ritual, such as vestments, plates, and amulets were retained— hence, the moniker, Ornamental Chamber. Poised at the entryway to the chamber are two great standing stones, eerily similar in type to *menhirs*, the monolithic upright stones commonly found across Europe and Asia that are markers of an important threshold. One of the standing stones dons thirty-two angles and attracts a crowd of gawkers who compete with each other to count the edges.

We follow in the footpath of the dozen or so people who meander towards the Inti-Huatana, known as the "Hitching Post of the Sun." Carved in the shape of a flat stepped platform with a protruding neck, this solid slab of granite is theorized to have been an astronomical calendar or clock. Strategically placed in a location where fixed points of the surrounding mountain range align with the stars, its emplacement on the landing most probably for observation of the celestial heavens at solstice. Ever mindful of the movements of the sun as the critical life-giver of heat and light, the Incas could have marked the sun's course by the progress of its shadow across the stone. Scientists have duly noted that the sun at its zenith casts no shadow on the Inti-Huatana, whose nickname the "Hitching Post of the Sun," derives from old folktales recounting the Incas attempt to tie the sun to this spot with a rope (Inti– sun/huata–to tie). Sizable enough to support a throne on its step, is it possible that a royal seat was offered to the sun as it passed over Machu Picchu on its daily course? Or was it the Sapa Inca himself who sat here to commune directly with the Sun God as he officiated over the Inti-Rayma (Sun Festival) held in the months of June and December?

The linkage to the sun as godhead is a recurrent theme throughout antiquity. The sun is the progenitor of growth, the source of relief from darkness, and of warmth from the cold. So, no surprise that the sun, at its rise in the morning and setting at night would be worshipped for the celestial benefits it bestowed. To associate the leader of a race of people to the sun was to connect to a divine source. Resultantly, numerous motifs of the sun as universal symbol of a king or monarch of an empire, as well as universal symbol of the godhead can be found throughout mythology. Hindus regard the sun to be the "First Cause of All Things," and regard its location at the center of the heavens akin to the heart as the center of the body. As the sun is the emblem of Vishnu, so it is to the Buddha; sometimes called the "Golden Man" or "Sun Buddha." In ancient Egyptian cosmogonic myth, the sun deity, or god *Re*, is storied to have traveled across the sky on a ship, descending into the underworld each evening and rising above at dawn as a daily manifestation of spirit. The sun as central to an origin myth is also referenced in Egyptian lore by the infamous pool of water at ancient Heliopolis where the Sun God Re was said to have bathed. As the story goes, it was from the murky chaos of this waterpool that rose a flowering lotus, the symbol of creation. Henceforth, the "Eye of Re-Atum" symbolized the sun and was attributed to be responsible for the birth of human beings.

Bolstering theories of the sun dial as a device for the surveillance of celestial bodies is a V-shaped outline on a forward ridge marking the spot where the Pleiades invariably appears during the month of August. This is a significant indicator furthering speculation that the Inti-Huatana was, indeed, an astronomical device. The month of August is the advent of Spring in South America, and the appearance of the Pleiades at this set point, would have been the signal for the critical time to plant crops.

Stefan and I carefully retrace our steps back to the central plaza, where a nearby trail leads to a cemetery. Here, Hiram Bingham discovered a plank of granite, so-called the Funeral Rock for its possible use as a table where bodies of the dead were dried in the sun and prepared for mummification. Bingham was also to find a number of burial caves containing skeletons, and noted that eighty percent of those skeletons were female. Signifying the presence of the Chosen Women, these remains have lead to much conjecture that Machu Picchu may have been a religious convent or monastery of some sort. Supporting this theory was American archaeologist, Paul Fejos, who in 1941 led an expedition to Peru. Rejecting the notion that Machu Picchu was a military outpost or place of refuge from the enemy, he theorized that the obscurity of the location was not pertinent to a military defense, but rather to prevent access to a sacred center by a non-neophyte—a parallel that would be analogous to the monasteries of Tibet and Meteora, Greece, similarly located on remote mountain cliffs. According to Fejos, the setting of Machu Picchu fulfilled three important requirements of an Inca monastery: (1) its landscape was a natural huaca; (2) its height and open view of the skies presented perfect conditions for observing the Sun, Moon and Stars, as well as the onset of lightning, thunder and the rainbow, all of which the Inca worshipped as emissaries of the Sun God; and (3) it could provide a safe haven for the Sapa Inca and his family to meditate and commune with the gods in solitude, while attended to by the Chosen Women.

Those called the "Chosen Women," the finest of those female virgins who dedicated their lives to the gods, and also known as the "Virgins of the Sun," are a key factor in comprehending the religious overtones of Machu Picchu. Homologous to the "Vestal Virgins" of ancient Rome, the Chosen Women dedicated their lives to the Sun God of the heavens and to the Sapa-Inca as his representative on earth. Schooled by the High Priestess of the convent (also known as the *mamacona*), these young women were carefully selected for their youth and religiosity, then meticulously trained to weave cloth, prepare food and drink, gather flowers and herbs, and most importantly, to cater to every whim of the royal sovereign. The

Chosen Women were also fierce protectors of their king, disposing of the cut hair and fingernails of the Sapa Inca in order to prevent their use for evil spells. Upon occasion, the life of a young virgin would be sacrificed, which was considered to be a great honor.

Of the 173 skeletons found in the burial caves by Bingham, 150 of them were women. Many were buried with the tools of their particular expertise; pots and dishes for cooking; needles of llama bone for weaving; and grinding stones used for preparing chicha beer. Distinguished from the conventional graves of the commoners and set high upon a rocky crag near the tallest point of the Machu Picchu peak, was found a burial cave that Hiram Bingham attributed to a High Priestess of some note. Evidence of her prestige were the precious objects she would take with her to the afterworld; fine pottery, tweezers and a sewing needle, two bronze shawl pins, the skeleton of a pet dog, and a concave mirror that may have been used for vanity purposes, or perhaps to reflect the sun. Awarded a burial site with a superior view of the entire city and the mountains beyond, this priestess must certainly have been an important figure.

Stefan and I pause to rest on the cushion of a grassy incline. I try to envision what it all must have looked like in the time of the Inca when over one thousand residents lived here at Machu Picchu. What was it like when all the buildings I now see were painted in the colors of the rainbow and covered with thatched roofs—and surrounded by orchids and the opulent life-size sculptures of solid gold and silver as described in the chronicles of Garcilaso de la Vega?

Stefan stares ahead in thoughtful silence. His hazel eyes pierce the air like a sword, as if trying to penetrate the mysteries before him. Minutes go by before either of us speaks.

"In the end," he says, "I find myself ambivalent to facts and data. Yes, I want to know, but I can live with the not knowing. In the final analysis, perhaps mystery is more delicious than knowledge."

"Yes, I think you may be right that mystery is more delicious than knowledge," I respond. "But I'm surprised to hear this coming from an astronomer, no less. As a scientist, aren't you searching out answers to the unknown in your work every day?"

A smile of admission crosses Stefan's face . . . and then a long, serious pause before continuing. "I suppose I am a scientist in dichotomy," he laughs, "Or maybe, it is more accurate of me to admit that I am just so frustrated that I will never really get to know this place."

· · ·

Fredrick and Jim are travelers from opposite sides of the world. Jim is a road builder from the plains of Edmonton, Canada, "where it's flat and cold," he says, and Fredrick is an economics professor from Munich, Germany. Fredrick and Jim have partnered together in that special bond of fellowship that only those travelers "roughing it out" in a foreign land can know so well.

"Come along, follow us," says Fredrick in the staccato rhythm of a learned and deliberate English. "It's an easy hike into town, just over the railroad tracks."

Located approximately two kilometers from the base of Machu Picchu, the town we're on our way to is Aquas Caliente, a small settlement built on either side of the rails that is maybe no more than a short city block in length. We have already caught a glimpse of its small shacks, fruit stands and open-air cafes on the train ride coming in. Named for it's popular hot springs (*aquas caliente*), the numerous pensiones located here attract those travelers unable to reserve a room above the cliff at Machu Picchu.

"Watch your step," warns Jim, "there's a gap just ahead." I do my best to keep up with the three men, skipping along breathlessly in my inadequate pink tennis shoes. Even though Aquas Caliente is impossible to miss, Stefan and I welcome the guided tour offered by Fredrick and Jim. We've been counseled that the hike along the tracks, with its missing railroad ties, sharp rocks, and potholes, can at times, be treacherous. I'm already finding it difficult to get a foothold; my feet sliding over mud and prickly gravel as we trudge blindly through the first of two train tunnels, pitch black to the outside world that waits in sunshine at its edges. Long drips of water leak through the ceiling, splashing on my forehead and nose as I fumble with the load of my heavy tote bag, reinstating the strap to my shoulder as it repeatedly dislodges itself. On through the second tunnel, I skip forward and scramble to keep up with the group—three fit and athletic men going along at a healthy pace. I was certain that the train was coming at any moment, which made for increased incentive not to lag behind.

Emergent from our passage through darkness, the great rapids of the Rio Urubamba rush past us in an exuberant tempo of energy; the velocity of its speed and intention offering a soundtrack to buoy our step. My spirits are bolstered by its unfaltering presence.

The monikers Rio Urubamba, Rio Vilcanota, and Rio Wilcamayu are all titles that may be used alternatively for the same body of water, giving rise to some confusion as to the distinction between the three. But in fact, the rivulet that cuts its path through the Sacred Valley is of the same watercourse that forms a triad at the northern territories of Peru, where it converges with the Apurimac and Ucayali Rivers at the Amazon basin. This upper portion of the Urubamba is sometimes called the Rio Vilcanota, most distinctly in the region of Puno, where it surfaces to ground. The term "vilca" (*wilca or huilca*) means "sacred" in Quechua, so it is understandable to find this appendage commonly applied to the name Wilcamayu or Huilcamayo (*sacred river*) at the section where the river runs through the sanctified lands between Pisac and Ollantaytambo in the Urubamba Valley. However, technically the entire snake of the river from upper to lower is that of the Urubamba, and it is not incorrect to call it so.

Arriving at village center, we dismount our backpacks and luggage to recover along the side of the rails, waiting thirty minutes or so for the one restaurant in town to open, but it never does. "Gringos!" come the excited shouts from a scattering of children suddenly appear brandishing bananas for sale. The band of three runs towards us excitedly, and when a young mestizo female offers me a banana for three cents, I give her a dime. "Damn it!" shouts Fredrick. "You Americans are driving up prices again!"

The broken down café we settle for is roofed with a shaky scrap of tin that is just barely held in place by the four wooden poles supporting it. Overly varnished and yellowing posters of Machu Picchu and Ollantaytambo are tacked with colored pushpins onto the only two cardboard walls. As a young boy serves us beers, his toothless mother banters about, enthusiastically playing hostess to her guests. When after a long wait the food is finally served, it tastes so awful that as hungry as I am, I find it uneatable. I push away my omelet and munch on a piece of bread. The high altitude has taken away my appetite, anyway. "My spaghetti is really quite good," says Stefan, but minutes later, he will get rather sick from it, and vomit.

Fredrick captivates us with horror stories of thieves in Arequipa, bomb threats in Lima, and floods in Puno. Floods in Puno? Apparently, the black storm we left behind in Bolivia had since raged into a devastating wall of water, raising the basin of Lake Titicaca to life-threatening levels and resulting in mass evacuations. What has happened to the floating islands of the Uros? The fragile reed homes? And the classroom with the old green blackboard?

A whistle blows, then a train whizzes by, sending flutters of air and dust through the open walls of our café. I brace my hands to the table and for a split second I wonder if the entire place will fall over. Sarah and Brad, a handsome couple from Australia who are traveling with their adolescent son, pull up chairs beside us. Describing themselves as flower-child hippies, they are ripe with questions about the Sacred Valley. Was Machu Picchu the legendary School of Idolatry where Manco Capac found sanctuary and religious instruction? Was it an elaborate tambo for the Sun God? A vacation home, as a local guide has intimated? Or a monastery of initiation? Long hours pass in conversation. Dusk has fallen, but we hardly notice. Soon, and without our realizing it, we experience a shift in perception that is without a sense of time or pressure. An easeful sense of belonging has crept in upon us. Succumbing to the comforting pastime of life along the railroad tracks, we have become as one with the villagers. Now, we too, stare transparently at the trainless rails upon which all activity revolves, spinning tales and shooting the breeze like old-timers practiced at our game.

Conversing of both the banal and the grand, from the minutia of the day's activities to the grand mysteries of the universe, we exchange sweet tales deep unto the evening hour. Who would have guessed, that here, in the shabby surroundings of a poor village named Aquas Caliente, we would have found our riches? I sit up straight in my chair with shoulders erect and breathe in the fresh air (filled with negative ions, some would say), absorb the sound of that great crashing river, the Urubamba, and take solace from the presence of the towering Andes looming above. Somehow, I feel better than I have ever felt in my life.

When at last, we tear ourselves away from the spell of life along the tracks to head back to our hotel, Stefan takes an unexpected detour in the direction of the hot springs. "I have a surprise for you," he says. I agree to follow his lead, having no idea where I am going while walking through a disorienting haze of complete darkness for several minutes. There are, of course, no street lights here and all around us is an unyielding blackness, save for a sliver of a waxing moon. In what is a spontaneous gesture, I find myself instinctively using my hands like a swimmer, as if to part the waves of thick air ahead of me. Looking foolish, I'm sure, I am distractedly "swimming" my way through the nightfall, when suddenly came visible a most beautiful sight. Foreshadowed only by a soft tapping that could have been mistaken for the chirping of a nightingale was a stone carver with mallet to chisel, chipping away in the solitary glow of an oil lamp. Defiant against the abatement of day, a luminous halo encircled his head, shining like a beacon through the black of night. Glimmers of the green serpentine stone he fashioned in his hand appeared translucent through the quivering flame of the lantern's light, so emphasized by the total darkness enclosing it. In a sublime moment of pause, that which was all other dropped away. I could have sworn that my knees buckled at the sheer moment of enchantment. It was an unexpected occasion of grace.

Stefan and I draw closer and respectfully introduce ourselves. Carlos is a mestizo of Spanish and indigenous heritage who has been carving in the tradition of his father, for all of his life, which I surmise to be no more that thirty-five years. He welcomes us with a smile and does not skip a beat from the purposeful sculpting of what looks to be a *Tumi-god*. From the far corner of the hut, a glint of movement discloses the presence of his family; three figures snuggling under a blanket and soundlessly peering out with shy curiosity. I almost don't notice them.

Speaking in my best traveler's Spanish, along with some sign language, I inquire politely if Carlos might show me his tools. He gestures towards a small table where a cadre of equipment laid spread across a canvas cloth. Handmade and so delicately wrought, the tools are much smaller than those I've ever seen before. Carlos hands me a rasp file and a scrap of crude stone, inviting me to give it a stone carver's try. It is unexpectedly soft and easy to carve. "Serpentine, found in the nearby hills," Stefan translates.

My eyes scan the assortment of sculptures hanging from the walls of the dimly lit shack, mostly comprised of little Tumi gods and big Tumi gods, with their axes of intricate relief work. The *Tumi axe,* or knife, is a ceremonial tool found in both Inca and pre-Inca convention with a semi-circular blade usually made of bronze, silver or sometimes wood. It is in this case, made of serpentine and is strictly an artistic representation. The handle of the Tumi knife is larger than its functional blade counterpart and is amplified by the image of a broad-armed warrior-god that brings to mind the weeping Sun God at Tiahuanaco. His elaborate semi-circle of a headdress is as much a denotation of his stature as it is a convenient grip for a handle.

If it be true that hanging a Tumi on your wall brings good fortune to a Peruvian home, then it must be so that the stone carver and his family reap the bountiful by the array of axes that predominate. When I ask if I might purchase a chunk of uncarved serpentine, Carlos is taken aback. He seems amused that anyone would want to buy a piece of stone with nothing on it, but before we leave, I do.

When Stefan and I re-enter the pitch black of night, we strain to see Orion and her Seven Sisters, but are hampered by the mantle of an overcast sky. A fuzzy image of a waxing moon lies on its back, as waxing and waning moons in the Southern Hemisphere are apt to do. The cloud cover of evening suggests there will be no sightings of Halley's Comet tonight—but one celestial event does not disappoint. I look back for a final glimpse of the stone carver's modest shack; the sparkle of light within now rendered by distance as one lone star in the night.

Stefan and I agree to retire to our respective rooms for a short nap, then meet outside at 2:30am. We will hike across the railroad tracks and then climb the almost six miles of mountain trail to see the sunrise at Machu Picchu.

14
ASCENT

The hotel clerk doesn't seem fazed at all when at 2:30am we turn in our keys and set out on a trek to see the sunrise at Machu Picchu. The sliver of a sideways moon is suspended in vagueness above us; uncertain through the murky pall of night and providing no benefit of light to our trail. It is so pitch black that we can't see the river, but the sound of its rumble commands the air. Stefan leads the way along the tracks with a pencil-thin flashlight that is our pathfinder. As we have previously noted three large gaps between the rails, we are extremely cautious, with each footstep methodically deliberated. Entering the first of two tunnels, I wonder if there are rats.

Some minutes, maybe an hour passes before we reach the bridge that leads to our ascent. The tracks were easy. This will be the hard part. Stefan and I agree to move along as swiftly as possible, in order to make it up the mountain before sunrise. I am more readily fatigued than Stefan, who has the endurance of a marathon runner, but I am equally determined and so my mind carries my body, pushing it forward.

At the elbows of the scissored footpath where we rest to catch our breath, we are bestowed with indelible views. The huge sugarloaf pinnacles of Putucusi and its brethren that in daylight commiserated in hushed conversation, now stand guard like watchtowers in the stark of night; their massive silhouettes black-on-black against the flat expanse of space. The half-moon soldiers on in its battle to perforate the mist and is caressed between the frame of two softly rounded peaks—and emerging from the earthly murmurs of the jungle below springs a horizontal row of buoyant pink clouds, releasing themselves skyward like helium from a balloon. "The pink clouds are lighter and therefore, rising above," explains Stefan, directing my attention to the surge of feathered billows, suspended in the air. Here, in the middle of the South

American cloud forest, the Ceja de la Selva, was this real? Or was it a deep, deep dream? It could have been either.

> Then up the ladder of the earth I climbed
> Through the barbed jungles' thickets
> Until I reached you, Machu Picchu.
> —*Pablo Neruda, Heights of Machu Picchu*

Sunrise is early in Peru this time of year and as the skies transition to a soft steel grey, we realize that the advent of dawn will occur before we reach the landing. As the climb has grown steeper and having just conceded defeat in the race against time, I indulge myself to rest on a granite ledge beneath a small waterfall. The cascade of sound is refreshing, although it's not possible to drink the water. Sitting there collecting my thoughts, I ponder the romanticism of the Incas, who stood peeled with anticipation for that pivotal moment when the great divinity would make its appearance at the crack of dawn. I imagine them at this critical point in time, festooned in their feathered headdresses, extending their arms upwards and throwing kisses to the sun, while I, on the other hand, relax on a stone, recovering my breath as the light unfolds around me without fanfare. Still, while no one is watching, in my own private homage, I blow a single kiss.

When we resume our journey up the trail, traces of Inca ruins begin to reveal themselves through gaps in the dense foliage. Like Rilke's breezes through the weight of dark matter, "ah, but the breezes . . . ah, but the spaces,"[4] they come as the rejuvenation of a fresh breeze, catalyzing us with a second wind as we stagger up the last of the testing incline to the crest of the ridge.

Gradient shifts to level ground and we are welcomed by the vision of a single llama, serenely perched in Buddha-style pose, just outside the Machu Picchu gate. With his huge bulging eyes and shaggy white coat, he makes picture-perfect subject matter for my camera. I cautiously work my way closer, aware of the rumors that llamas when agitated can spit like a camel, but manage to capture many beautiful photographs in the morning sun—all to the complete disinterest of the unfazed llama, who never flinches from his stance.

Morning has brought clarity over the range, and despite the fact that we have missed the drama of a sunrise over the city, we are recompensed by the gift of having Machu Picchu all to ourselves. It is absolutely still and there is not another soul here. Stefan and I agree to go our separate ways—he, on his grand exploration of the Main Temple, and me, alone to my wandering.

"Huayna Picchu? Huayna Picchu?" comes a voice, immediately breaking my respite of reverie. Where is this voice coming from? And who is it? "Phyllis, Phyllis . . ." I even imagine that I am hearing my name called. Is this possible? In the echo chamber of the Cordillera, sounds are multi-directional and sometimes phantom, so I am taken aback when it is a persistent guide dressed in a khaki park uniform who materializes at my elbow.

"Huayna Picchu? Huayna Picchu?" He repeats, with a question mark turn at the end of his phrase. I try to shake him off, but he stops me a second time.

"Yes, I see it. Huayna Picchu, I see it," I reply, nodding and pointing to the larger of the sugarloaf pinnacles.

"Huayna Picchu?" he nudges at my arm, again.

Okay, so I'm used to persistent hagglers and I know the game, but when Hectore (the name on his badge) doesn't give up, I relent and decide to appease him by following his lead . . . but only for a short while, I tell myself. It is with some reticence that I agree to let him show me where the trail to Huayna Picchu begins, but he misunderstands (or pretends to misunderstand) and before I know it I am plodding along a footpath to a little grass hut stationed in the middle of nowhere.

A gentleman in a baseball cap hands me a sign-in sheet where I am asked to write my name and the time of day. I take it that if you don't come down off the mountain, a search squad is dispatched, the prospect of which I have the luxury to find amusing, since I will not be needing their services today. After all, I had never really planned on climbing Huayna Picchu and I certainly don't plan on doing it now. Reaching the pinnacle of Huayna Picchu may be the aspiration of many a hopeful traveler, but it is not mine. I am not an athlete, nor a hiker with mega-tread outsoles. I am perfectly happy just looking at Huayna Picchu and have never considered attempting such a feat, most especially after having made the nightlong trek up the mountain. But here I was being goaded along, and for some strange reason permitting myself to be goaded. What happened to my trusty arsenal of New York defense mechanisms where I could just tell someone to "leave me alone and get lost"?

I'll just go for a bit, I tell myself, and then I'll turn around. I'll humor him for a while . . . then take off on my own. After all, this is my day of wandering.

The apex of Huayna Picchu reaches a height of over 8,920 feet above sea level and is 1,180 feet higher in elevation than the base of the Machu Picchu ruin site. There is no doubt in my mind that the view at the top has got to be an amazing panorama of the grounds. According to folklore, the peak of Huayna Picchu was the meeting place for the High Priest and Virgins of the Sun to greet the Sun God at dawn every day. The mindset that would have inspired the Incas to mount the pinnacle of Huayna Picchu and climb as high as any human could physically ascend in order to meet the sun halfway, seems a sweet and almost innocent gesture to me. Their effort to get as close to the sun as possible from the highest point on the earth that they knew is to be admired, but this should not be surprising from the same culture that threw kisses to the sun in an act of their devotion—and some might even say, love.

The trail begins with rock hewn steps that are sometimes substantial, sometimes crumbling into non-existence and sometimes growing to heights that legs are not anatomically made lengthy enough for. On these occasions, the welcome sight of a rope fastened with bolts into the mountainside provides us with the leverage to hoist ourselves up. The ascent begins so casually, having snuck up on me with its gradated steps, that I still have no idea if I am climbing Huayna Picchu or not.

"Is this Huayna Picchu, is this Huayna Picchu?" I repeatedly inquire to Hectore, who appears to have gone deaf and mute. At this point, it remains my disposition to saunter along for a while and then turn back. I still have no desire to take on the task of climbing Huayna Picchu, but I am feeling a bit disoriented as to where I actually am, especially since we have just trailed downhill into a dip, and then up again. I know that I am not on the face of a cliff, so this can't be Huayna Picchu, right???

Hectore keeps me moving at a drill sergeant's pace, waving his arms frenetically and never pausing for a moment. I guess if he never stops to look behind him, he never has to acknowledge my open mouth as it attempts to form a question between feverish gasps for breath. Perhaps this is Hectore's strategy for avoiding my protestations. It is working. Periodically, he leans back and hands me a tissue to wipe the sweat off my forehead. I am overheating in the alpaca sweater that mere hours ago provided much needed warmth from the chill.

The higher we climb, the wilder the surroundings get and soon I need all four extremities of hands and feet to claw my way up like a mountain goat—or maybe more like one of those lithesome pumas. The terrain turns perpendicular now . . . there is more hoisting, more footholds, more hanging onto boulders by the tips of our fingers. Slippery rocks alternate from damp and mossy to outright sopping wet; the trail sometimes widening into a quarried trackway and at other times vanishing to no trail at all. At this point, I highly suspect that I am on a serious climb here. I decide to confront Hectore. Hand on my hips; I plant my feet firmly to the ground and stand immobile, shouting his name until he turns around.

"Hectore! Hectore! Where are we?"

"Yes, yes . . ." he finally admits, "Huayna Picchu!"

I grit my teeth and try to be polite, ever cognizant that I am a guest in a foreign country. "Okay, very nice, Huayna Picchu. We come down now," I smile and nod, and smile and nod to no response. "Good, very nice. Done. No mas," I persist, my head bobbing in affirmation of the words that mask a desperate plea. But Hectore is either lacking of the English vocabulary or he knows exactly what he is doing. He turns his back to me and continues the march up. "Twenty minutes," he says.

Sigh! I am involuntarily surrendered to the situation by the sheer annihilation of any self-imposed will I may have had left. Now, I stop looking down and only look up. The view is dizzying, but somehow, I keep going. A group of four hikers pass our way, huffing and puffing and telling jokes about Inca elevators, everyone groaning in pain. I notice they are outfitted in sports gear and are wearing high tread boots, as contrasted to the dainty pink sneakers that I bought for the cute llama design on the insole.

"How much longer?" I ask.

"Twenty minutes," says Hectore, but he had said that twenty minutes ago. I begin to get it—that the twenty minutes is a ruse. It may have taken awhile, but I've got his modus operandi down pat now. I, in fact, may have been humoring myself along all this time as well, taking solace in an ignorance that is bliss and vacant of fear. Had I known that I was indeed embarking upon a climb up Huayna Picchu, I most assuredly never would have done it. Projections of impossibility would have created an impasse and deterred me from a feat that I would have not have imagined myself capable of. Perhaps the not knowing where I was going and what I was doing allowed me to be free from the struggle of a goal-set. I consider the possibility that I am acting out the template for a sensible way to live my life. Even still, as I move ahead, I never really expect to reach the top.

As we rise past a craggy outcrop of pointed edges, a small cave becomes visible. Its portal is so low to the ground that entering it would require lying flat in the graveled mud to slide my way through. Hectore indicates with a hand gesture that I should get down on my stomach, but I refuse. He is insistent.

"Is okay, is okay," he repeats like a mantra. I decline. And then . . . a crack in the veneer. Perhaps, it is because he won't take no for an answer. Perhaps, it is because I am swept up in the energy of the moment. Or more likely, it is because the lack of anything to lose has melted all doubt away. For without further hesitation, and without any assurance whatsoever of what may lie inside that small shaft of a cave, I acquiesce.

Preparing myself for the claustrophobic feat of entering the narrow inlet, I get down on all fours. The irony that the term cave is both a noun and a verb crosses my mind. The very thought that this hollow of a rock can also translate as the active verb "cave," as in succumb, surrender, yield, and defer, provokes incentive and transforms my mood. For all one knows, it is as in the case of the Neolithic tunnels of Orkney, where we are intentionally caused to crawl in humility before we enter the portal to another world, I tell myself. Outstretching my body level to the wet ground, I wiggle my way through the narrow inlet in the most awkward of positions, making silent apologies to my alpaca sweater all the while. I can barely see in the darkness, but it is within seconds that relief comes as the veritable light at the other end of the tunnel with the face of Hectore beckoning me on. Camera raised to capture the moment that I emerge; he snaps a photo of me in my vulnerable and disheveled state. I'm embarrassed at the unwelcome memorializing of imagery, but chalk it up to one more lesson in surrender (in this case, of all modesty) on my part. Hectore lends a hand to drag me all the way out. There is relief—and laughter!

From here on, the worst is over, as far as I'm concerned. Operating under the compulsion that nothing more harrowing than this can possibly occur, I feel a sea change wash over me. Now, I really want to reach the top of Huayna Picchu.

Catching up to the four hikers that had earlier passed us by, we cluster as a group in formation, alternately chuckling and groaning in chorus as we edge our way up the final steep grade. Walking sideways along a narrow ridge of the rock face, I am last in the chain-gang of hopefuls taking heedful steps around the bend when an unanticipated clearing of open space is revealed. The four hikers hug each other in celebration. Hectore reaches out to shake my hand and congratulate me. I'm happy, but confused. As has been my condition during this entire event, I still don't know where I am. Is this the top, or not? A piling of huge boulders above my head belies this clearing as namesake to the summit.

For the first time, I am the instigator and Hectore is the recipient. I nudge him on the arm and point to the next rise. In actuality, it is an assemblage of rocks stacked upwards from the clearing that represents what would technically be the utmost tip of the peak of Huayna Picchu. Now I know how Edmund Hillary must have felt in his compulsion to reach the zenith of Mount Everest. If I am climbing to the top, then I am climbing to the *real* top.

By the look of it, erosion has taken its toll and there is room for only one person at a time to take a position at the capstone. Hectore leans over and cups his hands like a stirrup, providing me the bounce to spring off my right foot and onto to the first block of stone that is my challenge. From there, I rely on sheer instinct to shift my weight and find a foothold. Attaching my body like Velcro, I embrace the boulder that is my barricade and literally throw myself over it. A fork-shaped log provides a niche for the next strategic point. Tenuous at best, its wobbly bridge provides no reference point to secure a forward step, so I half-climb and half-crawl the rest of the way on my hands and knees.

Exhilaration is met with a refreshing blast of cool air, drizzled with a fine mist of rain. As in a shift of perception where new visions are released to burgeon free, even the atmosphere around me has altered to a lavish essence. I have reached the crown of Huayna Picchu.

The writer and philosopher Goethe has said: "The highest a man can attain is wonder, and when the primordial phenomenon makes him wonder he should be content; it can give him nothing higher, and he should not look for anything beyond it." And so it is that there are no words recounted where time stopped briefly in my place at the apogee of wonder—and no need to look beyond it. I can only know in retrospect how all my senses pulsated as I melted into the 360-degree vista that both surrounded and filled me. The dizzying intoxication of the open sky, the heightened view of the huddled peaks, the panorama of terraced steps fanned out from the city below, the breeze as velvet against my body, and perhaps a condor or two overhead; all rendered me into a sublime state of presence. This was an experience I could return to through all the remaining days of my life; perhaps in times of need and by recollection altering my perception over and again like a laser beam of light piercing its way through a dark and tangled wood. From the corner of my living room on a hot California night, I will dream of these gentle peaks. I will listen for the sound of the Rio Urubamba; its music singing across my place on the mount. I will close my eyes and once again feel the soft spatter of drizzle upon my skin, and re-live the moment I sat victorious on the peak of Huayna Picchu. Always, I will know you, Machu Picchu, and in the memory of this moment, I will see you again.

Inca legend has it that the heavens and the earth existed simultaneously as one reality, the heavens being as real and as tangible as the ground beneath, with no division between. Some may call it the world of the wondrous, some may call it the fourth dimension—call it what you will, surely this place called Machu Picchu could convince us that it must be true.

. . .

By reason of its size, the large can of peaches that I purchase at the rest-stop near the entrance to the main gate would suffice a family of four. For me, it is my first meal of the day and the provender for an occasion of complete satiety. Indeed, when I arrive exhausted and damp from the rigors of the steep descent down Huayna Picchu, where I have half slid and half sat my way downhill while fending off the advances of a suddenly amorous Hectore, the offering of a can of peaches from a kind-hearted Peruvian woman is to me as a banquet sent from the gods. In spite of the fact that I have arrived at the open-air café too late for the daily-prepared meals, the shawl-clad gentlewoman, whose penetrating dark eyes bespeak her understanding, materializes a can opener, a spoon and a large can of peaches from behind the counter. She opens the tin and hands it to me, nodding her head in encouragement as I scoop a mouthful like a good patient dutifully swallowing the medicine prescribed to her. Without question, these are the most delicious peaches I have ever eaten—whose orange flesh and savory sweet juice are magnified by the setting of their occurrence and trouncing any of its kind plucked fresh from a tree. I slow down to relish each morsel, contemplating the irony of such impactful travel experiences as these that act as a vortex for the senses; siphoning in to their energy field something as ordinary as a can of peaches into the *extra*ordinary that from this day forward will be assigned to memory in confluence with the euphoria of having climbed Huayna Picchu.

An exuberant Fredrick ambles towards me with a spring in his step and takes a seat beside me on the stone bench. "Fantastic views on the trail to the Inca Bridge, cut in to the most glorious cliff-face," he recants breathlessly. "Just a narrow ribbon of a ledge between you and the gorge, thousands of feet below. Frighteningly beautiful!"

I recognize that Frederick has just experienced the power of a huaca. Indeed, such a vertiginous precipice would be regarded by the Inca as infused with sacred spirit for the powerful juxtaposition of its setting, as well as the dizzying visceral effect on the physical body. Frederick shakes his head in what looks to be a mix of bafflement and wonder. "I've never seen anything like this . . ." he mutters, as if to no one, "just never seen anything like this." Fredrick stares ahead into the vague distance. I join him. The clamor of the river below provides a white noise of static, its sound compressed by the canyon walls into a lulling backdrop to our pause.

I had come to Peru prompted by a photograph of a mysterious city. With a mere turn of a page in a magazine, a new bend in the road had unfolded before me, and I was compelled to follow it. But which has come first? The image as catalyst—or the inner stirrings that have risen to crescendo and step forward to be met? Certainly, Machu Picchu calls to many; a supreme mélange of human hand and nature at its most quintessential expression, its majestic beauty is as a spark that blazes into a dazzling fire; the perplexity of its very existence so powerful as to strike its beholders mute. As in the case of the unusual huacas that are deemed sacred by the Incas for their curious shape, so is Machu Picchu, as portraiture of form and space, distinguished for its romance. Surely, when we gaze upon it, we are elevated to a sense of the holy—that same angelic sense whereby the Incas blew kisses to the sun, and worshipped the moon, the stars, and the rainbow. Perhaps, like the Inca, we are moved in admiration towards that which remains elusive; beguiled by a powerful elixir of beauty and ambiguity that drives us to be relentless in our pursuit.

I reach into the back pocket of my jeans for the folded notepaper that I have carried with me throughout my journey. On it, I've written the same inspiring words from Rudyard Kipling's "The Explorer" that Hiram Bingham carried with him in his quest for the lost city of Machu Picchu:

> Something hidden. Go and find it.
> Go and look behind the ranges.
> Something lost behind the ranges.
> Lost and waiting for you. Go!

It occurs to me that Kipling's poem of an explorer on a quest indicates a sense of urgency—(*Go and find it . . . Go and look . . . Go!)* That which is hidden is without name in Kipling's poem, yet it prompts us to hurry. We do not know what it is or where, yet it waits for us to discover it—*(Lost and waiting for you)*—maybe just around the next bend.

But is it really hidden—or is it that we just can't see? It occurs to me that dreams need not be the exclusive dominion of the concealed where we delve to make discovery. Had the Conquistadors a keener eye, they might have deciphered the traces of a weathered footpath crushed into the flattened ground and spiraling its way up the rise to Machu Picchu; evidence of the inhabitants who tread upon it. Had they looked a bit closer, they may have discerned the shorn off twigs of the bush, intimating passersby. May it be the case that we are complicit in our puzzled trails? Perhaps, we see what we expect to see and what is regarded as hidden is merely that which has been obscured by our own belief about what we know. Perhaps, seeking a lost city is really a metaphor for seeking something intangible in ourselves that is close and ever present. Over the next range, around the next bend, we are prompted to forge ahead. We move with an urgency and with a passion. The beauty of an unearthed city calls out to us. We will never know it completely, yet we journey on. "Something lost behind the ranges" is waiting all the long while to be revealed.

Fredrick extends a vigorous handshake. He is off to see the Lines of Nazca in Southern Peru. "Good luck to you," he says, flashing a parting smile as he rushes off to get in line for the first of the minivans making the afternoon descent to the train station.

Left to my own company, the shout of the river sharpens into focus. Sometimes falling into the distance and other times magnified to the fore, the unbroken course of the river is signaled by the constancy of its roar. If it be true that the poet Ralph Waldo Emerson has said, "Good luck is another name for tenacity of purpose," then perhaps I might consider that tenacity has had a part, for I am struck by the irony of the river's resolve; the rhythm of its forward movement, unthwarted by the obstacles in its forward path. Over and around the jagged outcrops and boulders that would impede its way, impervious to what comes which way or that, the rapid flow of the Urumbamba is indefatigable in its course.

An orange dusk encroaches upon the range, and crowds of tourists, many of them day-trippers, gather cliffside to catch the next bus to the train station. I scan their faces, looking for Stefan who departs for Stockholm tonight, and am relieved when I locate him waving his arms wildly. He has secured a prime spot with the next group down the mountain and I decide to accompany him on the ride. Although I expect this to be an opportunity to catch up on the day's activities, we are otherwise distracted as our rickety bus tilts precariously at each hairpin turn; its speed exacerbated by the aerodynamics of a downward trajectory. A young boy sprints ahead of us on foot and amused passengers howl with laughter as we become party to an involuntary competition for a "first-place finish" to the train depot. The boy is winning.

The train comes faster than expected and as passengers scramble to get on board, it is with another hasty farewell that I make my goodbyes. Time slows and somehow this moment feels familiar, like *déjà vu*. A glimpse of my former dream leaks through

. . . I was standing on a dirt road saying goodbye to someone, but I could not see whom it was. There were lush green tropical mountains above me, and a muddy brown river below. The air was moist and I could feel it on my skin. Something about the dream consoled me, for reasons I could not fathom. I was on my way to something spectacular, the anticipation so great that a feeling of exhilaration charged through me like an electrical energy and stayed with me when I awakened.

Where was I in that dream, I had wondered? And what was I moving on to next?

"Safe travels!" I holler, competing with the blare of the engine as the train gears up to depart. Stefan pokes his arm through a window with a final salute, and I watch the train snake down the rails until I can see its image no more.

Word has it that in spite of patchy cloud-cover over the Amazon rainforest, sightings of Halley's Comet have been reported.

Quechua child on the steps
at Ollantaytambo

Llama at Machu Picchu

The peak of Huayna Picchu towers over the city of
Machu Picchu, as seen from the Watchman's Hut.

Close-up of an Inca wall at
Sacsayhuaman. No iron
tools or mortar were used.

Quechua child with her sibling at Pisac

The Sun Dial at Machu Picchu

Staircase at the Royal Mausoleum

A flight of Inca terraces

The snow-capped Andes as viewed
along the railroad tracks

Partial view of the zig-zag
trail to Machu Picchu with
the Urumbamba River
seen below

NOTES

[1] The Holy Grail is a receptive vessel of regeneration symbolizing the quest for purity and wholeness. The origin of the grail legend is sometimes associated to pagan Celtic lore, and in Christianity to the life-restoring chalice used by Jesus at the Last Supper. The quest to recover the Holy Grail is storied in Arthurian legend as the heroic journey of the Knights of the Round Table.

[2] "The Roads of Life" appears in *Out of Africa (From an Immigrant's Notebook)* by Isak Dinesen. First published by Random House in 1937.

[3] From *Inca Land: Explorations in the Highlands of Peru* by Hiram Bingham; Houghton Mifflin Company, 1922, original from Harvard University. Digitized June 26, 2008, p. 314

[4] Rainer Maria Rilke, from *The Sonnets to Orpheus*

ABOUT THE AUTHOR

Phyllis Mazzocchi is an avid traveler and writer who makes her home in Los Angeles, California. Born and raised in New York City, she received her doctorate in Mythological Studies from Pacifica Graduate Institute in April, 2011.

Printed in Great Britain
by Amazon